WILD LIFE PUBLISHING

"RAW MATERIAL...
ORIGINAL, THOUGHT
PROVOKING AND VERY
WELL PLOTTED!"
-TERI WOODS
NEW YORK TIMES
BESTSELLING AUTHOR OF
TRUE TO THE GAME

Promise

A BLOODY LOVE STORY

A NOVEL BY

NOW BORN

AUTHOR OF MOVING TARGET

PUBLISHER'S INFORMATION

Wild Life Publishing Presents
Promise: A Bloody Love Story

ISBN-10: 0692240047
ISBN-13: 978-0-692-24004-5
Library of Congress Catalog Card Number: TXU-888-797

Wild Life Publishing
P. O. Box 78964
Atlanta, GA. 30357

Wildlife.publishing@yahoo.com

Editor- in-Chief: Now Born
Editorial Assistant: Elizabeth Thomas
Cover Design/Graphics by Drea Delgado for KTL Graphic Designs
Paperback Design by eBookBakery.com
Manufactured in the United States of America

First Trade Paperback Edition Printing
10 9 8 7 6 5 4 3 2

AUTHOR'S NOTE

Dear Readers,

Hip Hop was my very first passion, and at the age of ten I began recording Hip Hop music. I came into the proper knowledge of myself at the age of 15 years old by way of the Nation of Gods and Earths. That's when I took on the name Now Born. Writing books was never a dream of mine, although the talent was dormant inside of me for many years. I can remember when I was in the sixth or seventh grade; I won a writing contest in my reading class. My teacher's name was Ms. Shivers. I had written a short-story called Ghetto Bird, a title which I had actually stolen from an Ice Cube song that was out at the time. Luckily for me, she probably never heard that album. From that point on, I hadn't attempted to write another story, unless it was in the form of a rap song.

I continued to hone my rap skills. I formed a rap group with two of my childhood friends, named Trav and Rampage. We were the original three members although, over the years, a few others have joined the squad. That group has been through quite a few transitions. I can barely remember the many names that we used in the beginning. For a number of years, we called ourselves Dead Poetz Society. While I was serving time on my first bid, the group made some recruits that I didn't agree with so I left the group. Trav decided to do likewise and together we formed a group called Wild Life. Rampage and I had lost contact for a few years because he was doing a bid. When we linked back up, he was doing his own thing but was still down to represent Wild Life because it was a family affair. The three of us were always like brothers from another mother. We never landed a deal with any major labels but we did a few numbers on the underground level. We were definitely hot enough to make it in the industry and we probably would have, had I not been so engulfed in the street life.

I came up in a good family, having both parents, and I also graduated from high school. For whatever reasons, I jumped off the porch at an early age. It wasn't long before I was robbing, stealing, hustling, smoking, drinking, and playing with guns. Those habits kept me going in and out of the penal system. I started out my last bid writing rhymes, an activity that I realized was futile since there were no studios or mic booths in jail. That's when I decided to experiment with this book writing thing. So I read a few novels just to get a feel of how these types of books were traditionally written. Then I brainstormed about what I could possibly offer the literary world that had not been done before. That's when I penned my first novel, a Hip Hop urban fiction that I called Moving Target.

For personal reasons, I initially released that book in my baby sister's name, Lavonda Wilburn. I'll explain those reasons in a non-fiction book that I'll be releasing soon, entitled The Fiery Furnace. My first thoughts were to submit Moving Target to a few big-named publishers, in hopes of attaining a lucrative publishing deal. My patience wore thin with that really fast and thats when I decided to go independent and start my own publishing company.

Rampage was murdered in April of 2006. Trav passed away in January 2012, leaving me as the only remaining survivor from the original group. When it was time to decide on a name for my publishing company, almost naturally, I selected the name Wild Life Publishing. That was my way of keeping their legacies, as well as my own, alive. I originated the name Wild Life in the early 2000's during a time when me and my crew were wildin' out in the streets. Now that Trav and Rampage are gone, I've gotta carry the torch for the team. On that note, I'mma say "Peace!". Wild Life Forever!!

Now Born

Acknowledgments

Let me begin by giving thanks to my wonderful mother, Nell Smoot, for instilling in me the will to always dream big and to pursue those dreams with every fabric of my existence. I received the greatest gift when I was born, and that was to have a mother like you. You are the epitome of strength, love and loyalty. Knowing that I'm making you smile and making you proud is my biggest motivation for going so hard in what I do. To my pops. You may not have been the best example for me when I was coming up but I know that, in your heart, you always loved us all. You were just battling with some vices which caused you to act other than your true self. I understand that that's not totally your fault, and I forgive you. I'm aware of the many snares that society has set for the black man. Therefore, I recognize that it's a shared responsibility. I blame the powers that be for creating certain conditions, but we have to blame ourselves for falling victim to certain temptations. To all of my sisters: Tarsha, Trina, Keisha and Lavonda, thank you for all of your support. To my nieces Timesha, Nija, Jayla, Nailah, Laiah, and my nephew Keyshawn; I'm encouraging all of you to keep those grade scores up because all of you are destined for greatness.

Thanks to everyone who contributed to this project in any way. To Drea Delgado at KTL Graphic Designs for the outstanding work that she always does when creating my cover designs for my books. To the amazingly talented author and close friend of mine, Joy Lowery, thank you for inspiring me. Also, to your mother, Mrs. Youndia Lowery; I fast and pray that you will be victorious in your battle against breast cancer, and that your years on this Earth will be many. You have a good heart and a beautiful spirit.

One Love, to my remarkable staff at Wild Life Publishing, to all of my distributors, and to all of my markets worldwide. Plus, I can't forget about the professional services of Michael Grossman at the eBook Bakery.

Peace to the Nation of Gods and Earths, and to Allah School in Mecca (Harlem), where I was privileged to learn the proper knowledge of myself.

A very special acknowledgment goes out to two of my brothers from another mother, Travis "Fresco" Kirkland and Lamont "Rampage" Clark. Mere words can't express the pain that I feel because you're no longer here. We had so much unfinished business and, when you left me, you both took a part of me with you. May you rest in paradise, and I will always keep your names alive through all of my works.

I would also like to extend my love to my friends: Ileia Belton, Shaquake Scott, Angie Morris, Shalonda Holmes, La La Bates, Latasha Gregg, Marquita Hall, Marketta Kelly, Porsha Kimberly, Kasheema Simon, Tamisha Holmes, Kimberly Jupiter, Jessica Johnson, Emerial Libby, Nicole Goodman and Melissa Tweed.

I can't forget about my right-hand man, Calvin "Victorious" Robinson. When I was behind the walls, you held me down like gravity. You're one of the realest brothers that I still have living, Word is life!

Big Ups to my cousins: Sally Pringle, Demetris Pringle, Al Green, Denise Keese and Teman Myers. Also, to all of my comrades: Andre Davis, King Justice, Demetrius Thomas, Jabbar Hart, Infinite Allah, Ty Equality, Tony Gusto, True Born, Shallah Marshall, D.J. B.I., Divine, Joey Scott, Shakene Richburg, Great Mind Allah, Tedrick Jeffries, Rev. Joey Nells, Supastar Ace, Ace Dime, DJ Prep Luva, Porta Rock Stax, Vincent Boseman, Julius Powell, Jethen Staley, Nkrumah Kirkland, Marcus Kirkland, Jamel Timmons, Andre Roach, Titus

Williams, Mckinney Hall, Robert Williams, Lenoxx Seventh, Steve McClain, Waverly Kennedy, Waleed Dubose, and Sintari Summers.

Most importantly, I want to thank you, whoever is reading this. And, everyone who purchased my first book, *Moving Target*. Thanks for your support.

CONTENTS

1

BLOODY MURDA

Murda and two of his partners had been torturing this kid named J.R. for three days. They had him gagged and tied up to a chair in an abandoned apartment building on Reisterstown Road. The word on the street was that J.R. had dropped a dime, and caused Murda's crack spot in Druid Hill to get raided by the feds. When the feds ran up in the spot, they found three black chicks cooking the work up. Two of Murda's blood homies were in the living room bagging up. Murda's older cousin named Cool was in the kitchen, keeping his eyes on the bitches.

Cool had just came home from doing a five year bid at Jessup, and Murda put him on as soon as he touched down. Everybody got bagged and the cops seized over $30,000 worth of coke and cracks. Plus they found hammers, some weed and a bullet-proof vest. It was over for Cool. He was on parole, and being caught in Druid Hill Projects was an automatic violation that would get him sent back to prison. Both of the homies, Redrum and Bang Bang, had priors so it was really a wrap for them niggas too.

Murda didn't really give a fuck about the three chicks. They were just some smokers who he had hired to whip up because they were pros at it. Plus, he didn't have to send his pitchers out on the block to give out testers. The girls were his own personal lab rats and all they wanted was to smoke as many rocks as they could for free. No smoking was allowed in the lab but, when it was time for the girls to knock off, these girls got higher than giraffe pussy.

The spot in Dru Hill was only one of Murda's crack houses. This nigga had work spread out all over B'more. He had a spot out in Westport, two spots in Cherry Hill, and one in Park Heights. The Dru Hill bust threw a major monkey wrench in his operation, but one monkey couldn't stop the show. This kid's money was long like a Stevie Wonder song.

Murda had a few of his goons to kidnap J.R. one evening after he knocked off work at the Rite Aid in Lexington Market, downtown. They snatched him up while he was walking to the Light Rail to catch the train home. When they took him down to Reisterstown Road, they tied him up to a chair in one of the empty apartments. Then they put a green handball in his mouth and tied a red bandanna around his face to gag him. When Murda arrived twenty minutes later, they started serving justice on him. Murda didn't wanna murk him just yet. To just pop his top would've been too simple. He wanted to drag him for a few days and really make him feel it before it was time to meet his maker.

First, he and his mans took turns beating him. One cat clobbered him with a metal Louisville Slugger bat. The other kid used a leather belt. Murda used a lighter and an oil sheen can to torch him all over. By day two, J.R. was looking like Jesus at the end of the Passion of Christ movie. Dry blood was all over him, dark wounds covered his skin, and he was all broken up on the inside. That's when Murda insisted, "Ayo, lets clean this nigga up!" J.R. could barely even move so they carried his limp body into the bathroom and dropped him into the bathtub. After taking turns pissing on him, they emptied twenty bags of ice into the bathtub with him. His entire body was covered, with the exception of his head. When they pulled him out one hour later, he had thick globs of snot coming out of both nostrils and he was convulsing violently. He was at the point where he was ready to die but Murda was having too much fun getting rec on his ass. After three long days of torture, the boy J.R. died and that was the end of his chapter. ❖ ❖

Murda had moved out of Baltimore about a year before all of that shit went down. He and his girl named Promise had a lavish 2-story pad out in Annapolis. Promise was a trophy chick. A dime in the face, thick in all the right places, plus she had goals. She was a jazzy redbone, real high-maintenance. Murda bagged her one day when he was dropping his little sister off at Prince George College out in P.G. County. Promise was a suburban girl, from Seat Pleasant. She was going to P.G. College, majoring in mass communications writing. Shorty was a writer; she liked to write stories, poetry and screenplays.

Murda kept Promise laced in all the hottest fashion: Prada, Fendi, Louis Vuitton, Dolce & Gabbana, you name it. He kept her draped in shines, plus he copped her a fly cherry red 3 Series Beamer. All the d-boys wanted Promise but they knew better than to try to spit at her. Murda was ranked as the Five Star General over a huge blood set in Baltimore called Billy

Bad Ass. If you make them niggas upset, you might as well just stop the earth from spinning and jump the fuck off. Since they came about, people started calling that city Bodymore, Murderland. They paint the town red for real and even the cops be under pressure.

Murda was a celeb around B'more and he really didn't give a fuck about Promise. He was a boss and he literally had hoes falling out of both pockets. Even though he kept her laced up, he talked to her like she was just a random chick; especially when his bloods were around. He did all types of things to disrespect her but she tolerated him because she had fallen in love with him. She was also reluctant to leave because they had a 2 year old son together named Zaire. Murda never really spent quality time with them. He was too busy running the streets, chasing paper and trying to keep all of his business intact. Plus, he had a full stable of other dimes that he would spend time and money on.

Deep down, Promise really wanted out of their relationship but she felt trapped with nowhere to go. Everybody assumed that she was happy without a care in the world, all with the exception of her best friend named Xena. She told her everything. Xena was headstrong, married to this army sergeant named Antiwan. They lived in Thompson Court on the Fort Meade military base. Their relationship was in stark contrast to the one between Promise and Murda. Antiwan was legit, respectful, and a damn good father to his two sons. He had a solid foundation while Murda's house was built out of straw and sand. All the feds needed to do was catch wind of the right information and his whole empire could've been blown away in the blink of an eye.

Meanwhile, Promise continued going to school and doing the housewife thing. She remained faithful to Murda despite his infidelity and disrespect. Little Zaire was her pride and joy.

He seemed to keep her mind off all the drama that Murda was putting her through, all the lonely nights and the rumors of other women.

Every night when she would finally get little Zaire to fall asleep, she would open her laptop and work on her book that she called Troubled Angel. It was her autobiography and she had been working on it for over a year. She would type until her eyelids became heavy, then call it a night. Murda would sometimes come staggering into the crib between 4 and 5 a.m. Other times, he wouldn't return home until the following afternoon. He would normally just grab a bite to eat, take a nap, take a shower, and then bounce out. They only had sex maybe once a week.

It was kinda odd that Promise had ever gotten involved with a drug dealer in the first place. Especially after the violent death of her father when she was ten years old, and the death of her mother when she was 13. Her pops was a local smack dealer who was doing his thing around Palmer Park, Seat Pleasant and Greenbelt. His name was Dontae but the streets called him Dottie. He was murdered during an attempted robbery in his home one night when he was there alone.

Promise and her mother, Treasure, had just stepped out to the Giant's supermarket to buy Dottie a case of beers and some food. Four burglars had been casing out the house for over an hour, waiting for Treasure to leave. They had no idea that Dottie was also inside. Their plans were to simply break inside, commandeer whatever drugs and cash they could find, and escape without leaving a trace. They had no intentions on killing anyone but two of them carried knives just incase Dottie returned home while the burglary was in progress. They knew that Dottie was dangerous and that they would've had to poke him out because he would've been willing to die for his.

The four guys broke into the house quietly, being mindful of the neighbors who might've been awake. Once inside, they heard music playing. They assumed that Dottie's wife had left the radio playing to scare off burglars like them. They crept inside and split up to search the entire house for what they had came for. Dottie was taking a hot bath when he overheard some commotion through the wall, in his bedroom. That's when he called out to his wife but no one answered. He immediately stepped out of the bathtub, tied a towel around his waist, and walked out of the bathroom to see what was going on.

When he walked into his bedroom, he found a young black man dressed in all black, rummaging through his drawers with his back turned. Dottie quickly charged him, tackled him to the floor, and the both of them began tussling. When the 3 others heard the ruckus, they all rushed in to help their partner. Dottie was strangling the life out of the young thug when another one of the guys struck him in his head from behind. Then, they all started stomping him out. Dottie put up a hell of a fight until one of the guys backed out a shiny butterfly knife and began plunging it repeatedly into his upper-torso. That's when massive amounts of blood began pouring from his body and there was no more fight left in him.

The guy that stabbed Dottie told the others that they had to make sure that he was dead before they left because he had seen all of their faces. That's when he passed the blood-soaked weapon to one of his partners and they all took turns stabbing his body, until all of the life had oozed out of him. The burglars escaped without being seen by anyone. They never found any money or drugs because they were all in a stash house that Dottie had across town.

When Promise and her mother pulled into the driveway, young Promise was the first to run inside. She heard the music playing because the burglars had left the front door ajar. She cheerfully ran into the house, yelling out to her father. When she walked into her parents' bedroom, she began screaming because the room was ransacked and there was no sight of her father. When her mother heard the outburst, she dropped the grocery bags and rushed inside. She immediately noticed the bloody shoe prints leading out of the front door. She yelled out to Promise and found her frozen with shock, standing in their doorway. That's when Treasure proceeded into the room and discovered Dottie's disfigured carcass lying in a pool of blood on the side of the bed.

It was a grotesque murder scene and the smells of blood and death tarried in the air. Treasure grabbed Promise and hastened out of the house, fearing for both of their lives every step of the way. Once they reached their car, Treasure sped nervously out of the driveway and drove to a nearby police station to report the incident.

Promise spent the next few years living with her mother, and Treasure never married again. Treasure was also a writer and that's what she did for a number of years to keep her mind off of Dottie. She was never able to get any of her work published so she eventually became discouraged and gave up on her dream. Money was scarce, their home was substandard, and she could barely even afford to feed Promise and herself.

The death of Dottie really fucked her up and she began using heroin after Promise turned 13 years old. After a few months into her addiction, she shot up some uncut heroin and it killed her. Promise discovered her dead body one afternoon when she returned home from junior high school. She was slumped over the kitchen table with a belt tied around her arm. There was a syringe next to her, and a beer top with a drop of water and heroin mixed in it.

Since then, Promise had been moved around from foster home to foster home. That lifestyle was compromising for her, but she was adamant about making something out of herself. Every night she would pray that her parents were together in heaven watching over her. One particular night, she made a promise to her mother that she would someday live out her dream of becoming a famous writer.

2

STRIKE ONE

It was around 3:30 one Tuesday afternoon when Promise and Zaire pulled up to the B Hive, pushing Murda's all red Acura TL with the brains blown out. The B Hive was a small pool hall that Murda had copped in B'more, off of Russelltown Road. It was a little lounge where his blood homies could go and chill, shoot some pool, and have some drinks. There was also a small room in the back where niggas would go and smash their little chicken heads at.

Murda had told Promise never to come down to the B Hive unless there was an emergency because he knew that other females were always commuting back and forth. Murda was always smoking dippers and shit so his memory was shot. He had forgotten that he had agreed to keep Zaire that afternoon while Promise went to school to take an exam. When she walked through the door, she was holding Zaire's hand. She saw a few blood niggas shooting dice, this bloodette chick was gritting on her from a distance, and The Game's song "Angels in the City" was blaring out of the jukebox. Murda was nowhere in sight. She only recognized one of the bloods, this chubby kid named Spark who sometimes came to their house to drop off money.

Promise approached him at the bar section and asked, "Have you seen Murda?"

Spark hesitated for a moment. Then he replied, "Bloody Murda stepped out for a second".

"Well, his Range Rover's parked out front. Who's he riding with?" asked Promise.

Before he could answer, this pretty young brown skinned girl came from the back room. She was dressed scantily in a short skirt and a halter top, and she was walking funny like she had just finished having rough sex. Promise began looking at her with piercing eyes so the girl screwed her face up and asked, "You got an eye problem bitch?"

Promise kept her cool and allowed the girl to continue out of the door. A few seconds later, Murda came walking out of the same back room. He was wearing a wife-beater, a pair of blue jeans, and some beef-n-broccoli Timbos. When he spotted Promise, his expression looked as guilty as sin.

"Murda, who the fuck was that bitch!?" yelled Promise.

"C'mon, don't come up in my spot lunchin' and shit. I thought I told you not to be coming down here."

"You're supposed to be keeping Zaire so I can go and finish taking my finals. I'm already running late."

"Well Promise, I'm sorry but that shit's gonna have to wait because I'm about to go and make this play. I can't have that lil nigga with me while I handle my scandal."

"Well, why can't that wait?"

"Because this is business ma, fuck outta here! I'll see you when I get home!"

Bloody Mary, the bloodette chick, saw the dispute so she approached and asked, "Murda, do you want me to fuck this bitch up?"

Then the two girls started arguing with each other. Murda broke them up and walked Promise outside, pulling her by the arm.

"Don't ever come down here embarrassing me like this again. Call that bitch Xena and ask her to keep him, I'm busy!"

Promise snatched her arm away from Murda, picked up her little man, and got back into the car to leave. The tires squealed as she murked off. Her eyes glazed over until she blinked one time, causing tears to fall from both eyes. She was embarrassed and swollen with rage as she sped en route to P.G. College. She tried to reach Xena on her jack but she never answered. Her only option was to take Zaire with her to school, and that's what she did. When she arrived in the parking lot, she was almost ten minutes late. She looked into the mirror and made sure that she didn't see any traces of her tears. Then she grabbed Zaire and hurried to her class.

When she entered the classroom, all eyes shifted to her direction and the room suddenly became silent. She walked over to her professor, apologized for being late and received her testing materials. The professor was still giving his briefing and the students had not begun testing yet. Promise found two vacant seats in the last row of the classroom, told Zaire to sit quietly, and tried to get focused so that she would do well on her exam. She had studied really hard and hoped that she could put her frustration aside until she was done testing. She didn't fret about Zaire being a distraction because he was always quiet.

The exam lasted for 45 minutes. She concentrated as hard as she could and she felt like she had done okay when it was all over. On the way home, she stopped by Chuck e Cheese. They ate some pizza and she let Zaire play a few games for behaving so well in the classroom. By the time that they returned home, Zaire was out of it so she carried him to his bed and he slept for the remainder of the night. Of course, Murda was out and about so she called Xena to explain how fucked up her day was. They talked for almost an hour, then Promise drifted off to sleep.

Around 8:30 Wednesday morning, Promise was awakened by a narrow ray of sunlight that slipped through the blinds. She rolled over, only to realize that Murda was not in bed with her. He had stayed out all night, once again. Surprisingly, Zaire was still knocked out so Promise went into the kitchen to whip up some breakfast. It was only a matter of minutes before the little man caught a whiff of the flap jacks and turkey bacon that were scenting up the entire house. That's when he came walking into the kitchen, rubbing the sleep out of his little brown eyes.

"Hey Za Za", said Promise as she smiled with her arms outstretched. The child then walked into her arms and she finished making breakfast. They were at the kitchen table, eating, when Murda walked into the house. His eyes were bloodshot as if he'd been drinking and smoking dippers all night long. Plus, he smelled like a fuckin' Jamaican club. Promise continued eating and she refused to say a single word to him. He proceeded to their bedroom and passed out at the foot of the bed. To clear her mind, Promise dressed herself and the baby, and they went out to do some shopping.

❖ ❖

Redrum, Bang Bang and Cool were all downtown Baltimore, sitting in the county jail for about 4 days before the feds came in to interrogate them. They were all being charged with manufacturing crack-cocaine, plus felony possession with intent to distribute. On the day of their arrests, Cool claimed ownership of the bullet proof vest, the weed and the two pistols that were found. First the fed agents tried to apply the pressure on Cool, threatening to send him back behind the g-walls for thirty years or better; day for day. They said that if he gave up his supplier he could walk scot-free on all charges. That shit went in one ear and out the other. Cool was as solid as a rock.

He was quiet for the entire interrogation and when it was over, he asked, "Is that it? I aint rattin' on nobody, eat a dick!". One of the two agents got all up in his grill, talking greasy and trying to provoke him to wing off on him. Cool nonchalantly gave an insulting laugh and said, "Stop the shenanigans white boy, you aint built like that. Bring me back to my cell". Then Cool walked out of the interrogation room and a white female officer escorted him back to his pod.

The next one to be brought in was Bang Bang. Off top, the agents noticed how young and green he looked. They had already read his criminal jacket and learned that he had a prior drug charge, but nothing federal. They offered him a Newport when they detected how nervous he was. Then one of the agents assured him, "We're here to help you and not to hurt you. We know that those drugs weren't yours because you only had $42 in your pockets when you got arrested. All you need to do is tell us who you are working for. We'll make sure that you get a bond, plus we'll pull some strings and see to it that you wont do a single day in prison. Trust us."

Bang Bang knew that he would've been a body in less than a week if he gave Murda up to the feds. He sat quietly for a few moments as the two agents stared at him like two thirsty bloodhounds. Bang Bang looked down at the tape recorder and said, "I don't know nothing. I wanna talk to my lawyer". Then one of the officers said, "Okay, it's your life kid. But, I wouldn't dare do 30 years for somebody who's paying me peanuts to do

13

all of his dirty work. He's gonna be out living the good life while you're growing old and gray in some shit hole out in West Butt Fuck. Suit yourself kiddo. If you ever change your mind, just give me a call or write me. And remember, there is such a thing as too late". The agent gave Bang Bang a card bearing his name and his contact information. Bang Bang was handcuffed so he slipped it into his shirt pocket and told him that he could return to his cell.

Redrum waived the interrogation process when the officers came into his cell. He knew the procedure because he had already done a bid once before. He wasn't working, he wasn't testifying on anybody, and he definitely wasn't about to give up his big homie Murda. He knew that Murda had him covered on the lawyer fees and all he wanted was a bond. His plan was to bond out and be on some gingerbread man shit, "Catch me if you can!" The feds normally only gave bonds to rats who were willing to cooperate. Other than that, you needed to have a damn good lawyer and your bond probably still would've been higher than a ransom. With Murda, money was no object. Redrum knew that as long as he didn't snitch, he would've been out eventually. Plus Murda would've made sure that he was put back on his feet and probably given higher rank in their blood set.

The three chicks who were arrested all planned to testify that they were only in the apartment buying drugs to get high with. They had all been arrested before for simple possession and crack paraphernalia like stems and shit. They knew that once the judge noticed all the missing teeth and how their eyes looked all sunk-in, he would've bought their stories. None of them had intentions of snitching on Murda because they knew that they too would wind up stretched out in some dilapidated building just like that kid J.R.

❖ ❖

Promise couldn't stand to be around Murda at all that Wednesday so she stayed out all day, bouncing from mall to mall. She went out to Columbia Mall, Wheaton Mall, Greenbelt Mall, White Flint Mall in Bethesda, and Dundalk Mall in Baltimore. She only bought a couple of outfits and sneakers for Zaire, nothing for herself. She mainly wanted to do some window shopping and clear her mind of what Murda was putting her through. When she returned home around 10:30 that night, to her surprise, all of Murda's whips were in the driveway and there were lights on in the crib. Zaire was sound asleep in his car seat so she picked him up and carried him inside. Four shopping bags were in her other hand.

Murda was sitting on the couch, watching the Knicks vs. Heat game when Promise walked in. She walked past him without saying a word, then carried Zaire to his room and laid him down. Next, she went into the bathroom and took an hour-long hot shower, hoping that Murda would've been gone when she finished. When she got out of the shower, she threw on a wife-beater, some pink boy shorts, and she wrapped her hair with a Louis Vuitton head scarf. Then she proceeded to her bed to get some sleep. Murda made that almost virtually impossible as he continually screamed on Lebron and Dwayne Wade through the TV screen. After about an hour, the game went off so he joined Promise in bed.

By then, Promise had managed to drift off to sleep. She was lying on her side when Murda kissed her on her face and said, "Bay, wake up."

She didn't budge at first but he continued to pester her, so she finally opened her eyes and asked "What do you want Murda? I'm trying to sleep."

He replied, "I just wanted to apologize for yesterday. I had to make that drop and I couldn't have my little man with me while I had drugs in the truck."

"Well, that's over and done now. I worked it out."

Promise rolled back over on her side. That's when he peeked beneath the covers and saw how juicy that ass looked in those boy shorts. He knew the pussy was fresh and he just wanted to bury his face in it.

He knew that she was upset but, at the same time, he was about to catch blue balls trying to figure out how to make her give him some. Then he got up on her real close from behind and put his hand on her thigh. When she didn't push him away, he took that as a green light to slide his hand up in her shorts and he started rubbing her clit with his middle finger. He could feel her juice box starting to get wet but she moved his hand and said, "Murda stop." That's when he begged her, "C'mon Promise, let me taste it."

Murda persisted until she finally gave in and let her shorts come off. That's when Murda spread both pussy lips and began licking on her clit. His mouth game was superb and, in only a matter of seconds, all of Promise's frustration had temporarily escaped. She moaned and squirmed with both legs spread-eagle, while her eyes rolled in the back of her head. He had her cumming all over herself. After he finished, she was so wet that he nearly drowned when he slid his dick up in it. He never really satisfied her when he fucked her, but his tongue game was official tissue. When he ran up in it and got his ball off, he only lasted in it for five minutes. As he was hitting it, he heard her crying softly so he asked, "Am I hurting you?" Then she asked, "Why are you doing this to me?", as a tear rolled down to her ear. For a second, he started going soft. Then, he asked, "Do you want me to stop?" "Just do what you want Murda", she replied. He didn't wanna pull out yet so she just laid there until he finally got a nut. That's when she put her shorts back on, rolled back over on her side and pretended to be sleeping.

As they both laid there in the dark, Murda fell asleep while Promise thought quietly about how she was gonna change her situation. She wasn't happy. It was 12:15 a.m. when Murda's cell phone vibrated on the nightstand. He woke up, realizing that he had just received a text message, so he read it. Promise opened her eyes but she kept her back turned as she waited to see what Murda's next move was gonna be. When she heard him place the phone back on the nightstand, she closed her eyes. That's when he leaned over her to see if she was still asleep. When he noticed that her eyes were closed, he went into the bathroom to take a shower.

Promise let the shower water run for a couple of minutes. Then she grabbed his cell phone to see who the message was sent from. Unfortunately, his security lock was on. First, she punched in his six digit birth date but that was the wrong code. Then she tried Zaire's birth date but that didn't work either. That's when the screen read that she only had one more attempt before the phone would lock and she would have to log back in through his email account. So, she placed it back on the nightstand and continued to play possum.

Murda got dressed and tried to sneak out of the house. It was almost 2:00. Just as he was grabbing his cell phone, Promise asked him where he was going. He said that he had to go to his trap out in Park Heights because he heard that someone had broken into it. She knew that was some bullshit because he was all fresh, plus he was wearing cologne.

Promise got out of bed and started raising hell. "Murda, you must think I'm stupid. I know you're probably going to see that lil dusty ass bitch from the B Hive!" Then he thought out loud, "Oh my god. Here you go again, on lunch box". She then stood in their doorway and argued that he wasn't going anywhere. Murda gave her a nudge and warned her to move before he got upset. "No!", she protested. Then he pushed her out of his way and walked towards the front door. Promise followed him, demanding that he stopped in his tracks and listened to her. As he was opening the door, she grabbed the back of his shirt. His first reaction was to yell, "Fuck off me!" When he jerked his arm back, he caught her in the eye with his elbow by accident. Promise tumbled to the floor as she bellowed and covered her face.

3

OPEN UP!

Promise balled up on the floor, laid there and cried for almost five minutes. Murda began apologizing and trying to help her stand up, but she angrily refused his help and demanded that he didn't touch her. Then she began reminding him that he'd always said that he would never hit her. He blamed everything on his reflexes, but Promise wasn't buying it. She realized that she was making a lot of noise and the baby's room was right above their heads, upstairs. So, she pulled herself together and walked to her bedroom. Her left eye was throbbing and the pain was excruciating. She could literally feel her eye swelling by the seconds and she was too afraid to see her reflection in the mirror.

Promise laid back down in her bed and curled up in the fetal position as she continued crying. Murda sat on the edge of the bed and tried to butter her up but she totally blocked him out. As Murda babbled on, all of Promise's bad memories with him flashed in her mind. Murda never got undressed and, after only ten more minutes, he asked, "Baby, are you gonna be alright? I have to go and check on this business". Promise didn't respond. That's when Murda kissed her forehead, exited the house and drove away in his Range Rover.

When Promise woke up around 8:00 the next morning, Murda still hadn't returned home. She had a terrible migraine; her left eye was black, swollen shut and she could only see out of her right. First, she went into Zaire's room to check on him. He was asleep so she went into the kitchen to take some pain medication. That's when she heard a car pulling into their drive-way. She didn't feel like seeing Murda, so she began making her way back to her bedroom to lie in bed.

As soon as she laid down, the door bell rung. She ignored it until it rung a second time, and her cell phone rung simul-taneously. She squinted painfully as she struggled to make out the caller's name on her screen. When she realized that it was Xena, she answered in an exhausted voice.

"Wake up girl, I'm out front. Open the door", said Xena in her normal happy-voice.

Promise felt so ashamed that she denied her, "Not this morning Xena, I'll just call you later".

"What? I just drove all the way from the base girl. Are you alright?" "I just aint pressed for company this morning," said Promise just before hanging up on her.

Xena could sense that something was wrong because this was definitely abnormal behavior. They were so much in tune with each other that Promise couldn't fake it even if she tried. Xena continued ringing the doorbell and knocking because she started to fear that her best friend might've been in danger. Promise stopped answering her cell and that's when her spider senses really started tingling. Then she yelled out, "Promise I'm calling the cops if you don't open this door. I know something is wrong in there!"

She believed that Murda was probably inside beating on her or something, because she knew how much of an asshole he was. She hated that nigga and always tried to persuade Promise to find someone better.

Promise didn't want Xena to awake the baby. Neither did she want for the cops to come to their home and see her face because Murda would've been arrested without a doubt. Promise walked back to the door and said, "Xena everything is fine, just go."

"I'm not leaving until I see your face and know that you are truly okay."

Promise became silent and stood there for almost thirty seconds without opening the door. After Xena cried out to her once more, Promise demanded, "Promise me that you won't over-react if I open this door".

"I promise...just open up."

Xena's heart fell to the floor when Promise opened the door. She welcomed her inside, demanding that she toned her voice down so that she wouldn't wake up Zaire. Xena's blood almost came to a boil as Promise explained the incident just the way that it happened. She stressed the fact that she didn't want the cops involved. She also said that the pain wasn't as severe as it looked. Xena kept arguing that Murda wasn't shit and that Promise could find someone better. Then she suggested that Promise packed her things at that very moment, and came to stay with her and Antiwan. Promise declined the offer, and insisted that she was okay.

Promise thought about the fact that Zaire would definitely be awake soon. That's when she asked Xena to babysit him for a few days because she didn't want him to see her with a black eye. Xena agreed so Promise packed his bags and carried them outside to Xena's car. Xena got Zaire out of bed without awaking him. Then she carried him to her car.

Promise watched through the kitchen window as Xena drove away. She wasn't worried about Zaire wilding out because he loved being around Xena's two sons. They were both older than Zaire but they all got along fine. As Xena's car disappeared in the distance, Promise made her way to the freezer to make a homemade icepack. She put five ice cubes inside of a face cloth and placed it on her eye, in hopes that the swelling would go away.

❖ ❖

Almost two weeks had passed since the Dru Hill bust. Bang Bang stressed in his cell day and night, frequently staring at the card that the agent had slid into his shirt pocket. The director over the Baltimore City Jail had niggas on some real Guantanamo Bay shit. That was his method of coercing people into pleading guilty so that they could hurry up and get sentenced, and then get shipped to another institution where the living conditions were better.

Bang Bang's sink didn't work, the meals were skimpy, the toilet barely flushed, plus the heat stayed on full blast 24/7. His cell was so hot that even the floor and the walls were sweating. His cellie was a Spanish cat named Joell. He was federal too, but he had turned state and was about to get released in a couple of weeks. He had framed this brick nigga named Rico from West Baltimore, and he was waiting to testify against him in two weeks.

As Bang Bang paced back and forth in the sweltering heat, Joell kept recommending that he did the same thing. Bang Bang was leery about that because he knew that the feds played a dirty game. He felt like they would've let Joell testify and still sent his ass to some fed joint out in the mountains somewhere.

Plus, he knew that the witness protection program was some bullshit, and so was the whole confidential informant deal. As soon as he would've signed that statement, the streets would've known.

Cool and Redrum kept it all the way gangsta. The thought of ratting never once entered their minds. The three of them were all assigned to separate dorms so they had no means of communicating with each other. When Cool and Redrum made their collect calls, their girls told them that Murda had contacted them and was working on getting them a bond. He had a blood homie who was a bail bondsman but the judge hadn't given either one of them a bond yet. Murda also had his own personal lawyer looking into their situations to see if he could spit at the judge and get their bonds set. He gave each one of their girls $500 to put on their books too.

Bang Bang's girl was a scumbag bitch but Murda didn't know it. He should've put the bread in somebody else's hands because she cuffed it and didn't send Bang Bang one red cent. She wasn't even accepting his collect calls. He had spent the $42 that he got bagged with during his first week, buying snacks from the canteen. He ran through that in about 3 days. Meanwhile, Cool and Redrum had snacks on deck, bidding comfortably.

❖ ❖

Murda's Range pulled into the driveway around 4:15 p.m., almost six hours since Xena had left with Zaire. Promise had cleaned the entire house. She was sitting at the kitchen table, typing her book on her laptop, when Murda walked in. She had her hair styled with a bang covering her left eye. Murda placed his hands on both of her shoulders from behind and kissed her cheek. She noticed the fragrance of a female's perfume coming from his shirt. Murda had derailed her whole train of thought and broken her concentration, still she pretended to be focused on her work. That's when Murda proceeded to the bedroom, took off his jewels, emptied his pockets and passed out on the bed.

After an hour of straining to get back focused on her book, Promise shut off her laptop. She went into the kitchen and rubbed some butter across her bruised eye because that was an old home remedy that she remembered learning from her mother. She called Xena and spoke to Zaire for a minute. Then she watched Tyler Perry's, *Daddy's Little Girls* until she got sleepy.

Around 8:00, she walked into the bedroom. Murda was lying on his back and snoring like he weighed three hundred and fifty pounds. Promise walked over to the nightstand and turned on the lamp so that she could grab her headscarf out of the drawer. That's when she noticed Murda's things on the nightstand: his Presidential Rolex, a gold 40-inch cable with a Jesus piece, his bankroll, his cell phone, a box of Newport 100's, and a book of matches.

Promise was tempted to try and crack the code to his cell phone's applications but something else caught her eye. She saw the symbol on the book of matches, a pink flamingo. She recognized the symbol from a TV commercial that was advertising a strip club called Flamingos, located downtown Baltimore on Baltimore Street. That's when she realized where he'd been going every night. She couldn't believe it, as beautiful as she was. Plus she was a good woman. *What the fuck could he be searching for in a strip club?*

Promise laid down alongside Murda and turned the lamp off. For a while, she just laid there, staring angrily at his figure in the dark. Then she closed her eyes, silently recited the serenity prayer and an original prayer to God, her mother and her father. That gave her the solace that she needed to finally fall asleep. When she awoke on the next morning, the pain had subsided and so did the swelling. Her mother's old remedy must've been working. When she noticed how bright the sun was shining, she promised herself that she wasn't gonna let anything stress her out that day. Murda was still asleep so she went into the bathroom to freshen up. Then she ate a fruit salad for breakfast and went online to find out the scores to her final exams.

When Promise learned that she had aced all of her exams, and that her lowest score was a 94, that gave her an even greater boost to jumpstart her day. That's when she parked in front of her laptop and knocked out an entire chapter by noon. She had some inspirational Jill Scott songs playing on her Windows Media Player for the entire time that she was typing. Then she decided to put on one of her best outfits and take a solo ride on the town.

She threw on an all-black Roberto Cavalli dress that hugged her coke bottle frame like a glove. Plus a fly pair of Christian Louboutin open-toed stiletto sandals to show off her French pedicure. She combed her silky black hair down into a wrap and grabbed her all-black Marc Jacobs clutch bag. Then she posed in front of the mirror in Zaire's room and realized how stunning she looked, despite the black eye that she had. Of course, she had a solution for that too. She threw on her Tortoiseshell Versace shades. Then she took a second look in the mirror, smiled confidently, and recited a mantra that her mother always used to say. "I'm too blessed to be stressed, and too anointed to be disappointed."

She left Murda's trifling ass sleeping in bed, grabbed the keys to her 3 Series, and left without saying a word to him. As she backed out of the driveway, she flipped through the local radio stations to find some good tunes to keep her spirits up. When she turned to WPGC, they were playing some go-go bullshit so she switched to 92Q. They were playing some down south crunk shit and that wasn't about to get any burn in her ride either. That's when she just popped in a gospel mixed CD, let the a/c pump, and jumped on highway 50.

Promise was really zealous about her test scores and also the progress that she had made on her book. She wanted more inspiration to continue writing so she decided to visit her old neighborhood in Seat Pleasant and reflect back. She drove past her elementary school, the neighborhood park where she used to play, and the house that she grew up in. The memories that came to mind were somewhat painful but also reminiscent of just how strong she was and how much she'd endured in her past.

Pretty soon, she became hungry so she drove to one of her favorite restaurants called Jaspers Fish and Grill out in Landover. After filling her belly with some of the best seafood that money could buy, she returned home to resume working on her book. Her day was going great, and she felt even better when she arrived at the crib, only to find that Murda wasn't there. "Finally, some peace of mind", she thought. Zaire was gone, Murda was gone, and her creative juices were flowing. She called Xena's house and spoke to Zaire for a short while, assuring him that she would be coming to pick him up in a few days. Then she cranked the Jill Scott back up, poured herself a glass of White Zinfandel and began typing whatever memories came to mind.

4

THE STRAW THAT BROKE
THE CAMEL'S BACK

It took an entire week for Promise's eye to heal. The black ring had disappeared but there was still a blood clot near her cornea. That's when she decided to go to Fort Meade to pick up her son. When she arrived at the military post, the M.P. wouldn't let her enter the base because she didn't have a military I.D. So, she called Xena and she brought Zaire to her. Zaire was happy as hell to see his mother and she was even happier to see him. She was missing him like crazy for that entire week.

Murda stuck to his normal routine; keeping business and pleasure as his first priorities, family being his last. Troubled Angel was almost completed and that became Promise's tunnel focus, publishing her book and fulfilling the promise that she had made to her mother. When Murda stayed out all night, she really didn't even give a fuck anymore. She had already decided that once she got her book published, and got her own website jumping so she could promote it and generate some sales, she was gonna leave his ass. Right now, she didn't have any means of getting paid, besides the money and make-up gifts that she often received from Murda.

❖ ❖

On this particular Thursday night, Promise and Zaire were home alone while Murda was out, supposedly handling some important business. It was almost 2:00 a.m. when Promise was awakened by some noise coming from downstairs. At first, she thought it was Murda just being inconsiderate like he often was when he would return home high off dippers. He would come home while she was sleeping, turn on the bedroom light, listen to loud music downstairs, and do all types of superfluous nonsense. But, this wasn't the case tonight, and it dawned on Promise when she heard the sound of glass breaking and the whispers of what sounded like more than two people downstairs. Right then, she realized that she had just had a nightmare about the night when her father got murdered.

Promise began to panic. Her first instinct was to go for Murda's Hi-point .380 that he kept stashed under the mattress on the side of the bed that he normally slept on. Then her motherly instincts kicked in and she crept out of the room as quietly as she could, heart racing and worried sick. As she got closer to Zaire's room, the voices downstairs became more audible. One voice kept whispering, "Shhh... shut the fuck up!" That's when she knew that something wasn't right. When she peered into Zaire's room, he was sound asleep so she shut his door and walked closer to the staircase to make sure that Murda wasn't the one making all of the commotion. Just as she was about to walk down the stairs, she noticed a man dressed in all-black, making his way up the stairs.

She yelled out and he froze like a deer in some headlights after noticing the black pistol in her right hand. Out of fear, she trained the gun in his direction and squeezed the trigger. Then, Bong! Bong! Promise caught him once in the arm and he bolted out of the front door. He ran so fast, you would've thought that nigga was Seabiscuit. She noticed two more men following his suit, both empty-handed. A few moments later, she heard two car doors slamming and the sound of tires screeching outside, assuming that was them making their getaway.

Before proceeding downstairs, she grabbed the phone off the wall at the top of the stairs and dialed 911. When the dispatcher answered, she whispered into the receiver, "I'm being robbed, please help me". Then she left the phone off the hook, hanging by the cord. She began panting and sweat pellets formed across her forehead as she took baby-steps down the stairs. The hot pistol was burning her palm but she was too afraid to let it go. She was almost certain that the burglars were all gone because the commotion had ceased. There was a dead silence throughout the house, except for the sound of a few cars passing by because the burglars had left the front door open.

Promise reached the bottom of the stairs and turned the corner with her pistol in hand. She held the gun with both hands and held it close to her chest, similar to a midget at the steering wheel. There were no more burglars in sight but the living room was a wreck and most of the electronics were missing. Zaire's Wii video game, the flat screen, the stereo system, the DVD player, and the monitors for the surround sound. Promise then closed the door and locked it. The burglars must've been in the house for a while because they had taken all of the wires, RCA jacks, and everything. Plus, they must've made a few trips back and forth to the car because they all left empty-handed when Promise started dumping on 'em. Those greedy bastards even stole Zaire's penny jar, which probably had a couple of hundred dollars in change.

Then it struck her..."My laptop!" she yelled as she hurried to the kitchen which was also located downstairs. She ran into the kitchen and the light was turned off. When she turned it on, there it was. Her laptop was sitting on the tabletop, obviously untouched. She repeatedly tried to call Murda and inform him of what had happened. Her calls all went unanswered, and she could've sworn that he forwarded her twice. She was about to leave a voice message until she was startled by the ringing of her doorbell.

After noticing the red, white and blue police strobes flashing through the blinds, she opened the front door and invited the cops inside. They arrived three police cruisers-deep, all Caucasian men. The officers took about a half hour to write up the incident report.

Promise told them that the burglars never made it upstairs and she kept the light over the staircase turned off. She did that because she didn't want them to walk upstairs and notice the bullet-hole in the wall, and the small amount of blood that the burglar had leaked on the carpet of the stairs. She never mentioned that she had shot anyone because she knew that Murda's gun wasn't registered. The serial number was scratched off and everything. Promise told the officers that she didn't feel safe, and she asked if they would stay with her until she packed up a few things for herself and the baby. Two of the squad cars left, while one officer waited about ten minutes for Promise to gather her things. Then she left, initially, to look for a suitable hotel. By then, it was approximately 4:00 a.m. Murda still wasn't answering his jack, and Promise was starting to get real heated. "What if I would've woke up five minutes later than I did?" she considered. She and Zaire could've both been killed.

It had been years since Promise had slept in a hotel room and she had no clue of where to begin her search. She tried to call Xena but her phone was turned off for the night, probably being charged.

Promise looked back at Zaire who was asleep in the back-seat, unfazed by the whole situation. He was totally oblivious to everything that had transpired. Thats when Promise decided to take a little trip to downtown Baltimore, to see if she would find Murda tricking off at the Flamingo club. When she arrived at the club at approximately 5:00, sure as shit, his Range was parallel parked not very far from the club's entrance. Knowing that she couldn't take Zaire inside, she decided to wait in the car until Murda walked out. She kept blowing up his phone but he still wasn't picking up. The sun would've been rising in about an hour so she knew that it wouldn't be much longer before he walked out.

After about twenty minutes, a tall blonde-haired white woman came walking out of the club. She was a dime for a white chick, resembling Amber Rose in the face. She was carrying a gym bag. Promise assumed that she was a stripper from the way that she was flaunting her assets in her skimpy outfit. Still, there was no sign of Murda. The woman seemed to be walking towards Murda's passenger door and that's when Promise tried to zoom in, wondering if Murda had been waiting in the Range for the entire time. The woman then whipped out a set of keys from her purse and pressed the button to deactivate the car alarm. She placed her bag in the passenger's seat, then walked around the front of the truck and hopped into the driver's seat.

Promise started feeling really stupid after realizing that she must've mistaken this woman's truck for Murda's. Then she started her car and began driving in the same direction as the white woman. She was tired as hell and, at that point, she couldn't care less about which hotel she went to. As she got closer to the Range Rover, she noticed a distinctive small red 5-pointed star that Murda had placed in the bottom-right corner of his back windshield. That's when she realized that this was definitely Murda's truck.

At that moment, she became wide awake and eager to find out who was this white bitch pushing her man's whip. Promise had the rams. She got so hype that you would've thought she just popped a couple of horny goat pills. The white woman pulled into a nearby Seven Eleven, and Promise turned in right behind her. The woman parked the Range so Promise parked in the back of her, blocking her in. Then she approached the driver's side of the truck, as the woman was fumbling through her purse. On her way over, she noticed an empty car seat in the backseat. Then she began questioning herself, "Could there possibly be another Range in this city with that same distinctive red sticker?"

Promise tapped on the woman's window and almost made her shit in her panties. The window was cracked so Promise started talking real aggressive-like. All of that suburban girl shit went out the window and you would've thought that Promise was straight outta Compton or somewhere.

"Look bitch, I don't know you and you don't know me but if this is my truck you're driving, I'm about to kick your little stripper ass all over this parking lot!" she threatened.

The woman replied, without opening the door, "I'm sorry but apparently you've got the wrong truck".

"Well open the door, let me talk to you!" said Promise as she tried to open the door from the outside. It was locked so Promise began making more threats and calling her everything but a child of God.

After realizing that she was blocked in, the woman grabbed her cell and made a call. After only a few seconds, a Baltimore city police car pulled into the parking lot. The officer was this old gray-haired Bob Barker looking ass white man. He stepped out of the car, seemingly taking sides with the white woman off top. Promise was trying to explain that the woman was driving her truck but the officer kept asking for her I.D. as if she was in the wrong. It wasn't until a second officer showed up that Promise was really allowed to state her case. That officer was a younger black man.

Now that police were on the scene, the woman found the courage to step out of the truck and she began explaining her side of the story to the white officer.

"Officer, I've never seen this woman. I believe that she was trying to rob me before you arrived. This truck belongs to my babies' father and I can call him right now to prove it", she explained.

"That won't be necessary, just relax. I believe you", he replied.

As Promise was explaining her side of the story to the black officer, Bob Barker interrupted her and threatened, "Ma'am, don't you know that you can be charged with assault, attempted robbery, and possibly kidnapping for blocking her in with your car?".

As he started to continue on, the black officer interjected at midsentence, "Hold on Wilson, I just ran the tags and this truck is registered in this woman's name."

The other officer's jaw dropped, as if to say, "How the fuck could this fuckin' black monkey afford a Range Rover and a 3 series BMW?"

Then all three of them walked back over to the white woman and told her to explain her case once again because she was now in danger of going to jail for stealing the truck.

She explained, "My babies' father told me that I could drive this truck to work last night and I had no idea that it was stolen."

The white officer was acting like he didn't wanna take this white bitch to jail and he calmly asked her, "Ma'am, what's your babies' father's name and where is he now?"

She answered, "His name is Joseph Reed and he's at our house on Emerson Avenue, probably getting our oldest son dressed for school. I was on the way to take him this truck so he could take him to school by 8:00."

When Promise heard the name Joseph Reed, she almost went into cardiac arrest because that was Murda's government. She asked, "Your son? What the fuck do you mean, your son? Bitch, that's his only son in the backseat of my car!"

Both ladies seemed shocked at what they were hearing, but Promise was ready to smack this woman's head clean off her shoulders. If the cops weren't there, it would've been ugly.

The black cop asked Promise, "Do you want this woman arrested?"

Promise felt a burning sensation rising in her chest as she stared angrily at the other woman, deciding on her fate. What burned even more was the curiosity to know was this woman telling the truth. That's when she reasoned, "If she can prove right now that Joseph gave her permission to drive it, she's free to go. But if not, I want her arrested for car theft."

The woman reached for her cell phone, seemingly confident that Murda was about to pick up. She turned on the speakerphone as soon as she dialed his number, and it started ringing. After only two rings, a young boy answered, "Hi mommy". She giggled, gave Promise a condescending smile and said, "Hey J.J., let me speak to your father hun". A few seconds later, Murda's voice came through the speaker and Promise's heart practically locked upon her. She was appalled at the fact that her call had went straight through, first of all. She couldn't believe what she was witnessing; Murda had been living a double life the entire time. Needless to say, Murda co-signed everything that the white woman had told the police. She never mentioned to Murda that she had met Promise, and Promise remained silent until the duration of the call.

5

FED UP

Promise found out that the white woman's name was Winter. She and Promise realized that their beef wasn't with each other. Murda was the master puppeteer, playing them both like puppets on a string. Winter told Promise that she and Murda had been together for over 5 years and that they had two sons together. The youngest, Josiah, was two years old. He was born during the same month and year as Zaire. The oldest son's name was Joseph junior, aka J.J. He was going on 5 years old. They owned an all-brick two-family dwelling together on Emerson Avenue in B'more, even though no other family lived there. The crib was decked out just like the one that he and Promise shared in Annapolis.

Promise told Winter that she was done with Murda. This was the straw that broke the camel's back. She just wanted to go back and pick up the rest of her things, then leave his ass. Winter didn't seem as upset as Promise did. She probably felt like Promise had been played the worst, knowing that Murda always spent his nights with her and their two sons.

They spent almost twenty minutes in the Seven Eleven parking lot, talking, before Winter realized that her oldest son would be late for school if she didn't hurry home. That's when Promise told her to go ahead and drive the truck home, and that it was her choice whether or not she decided to tell Murda that they had met. Promise didn't feel the need to say anything to him because her dealings with him were over as far as she was concerned. When Promise got back into the car, she called Xena's cell. It was around 7:30 so she figured that she'd be up, probably walking her sons to their bus stops.

"Hello", Xena answered.

Promise began, "Are you busy right now?"

"Not really, why?"

"I'm leaving Murda. I need to know if Zaire and I can stay with you and Antiwan for a little while, just until I can scrape up enough money to get my own apartment."

Xena said "Of course, but what happened sis?"

"I'm just fed up with this nigga", Promise exclaimed, getting teary-eyed. She told her about the burglary incident and what she had found out about Murda's other children.

When Xena returned home from the kids' bus stops, she woke Antiwan up and they both rode out to meet with Promise in Annapolis. They met up in a McDonald's parking lot because Promise was too afraid to go back to her house alone. When they arrived at her house, Murda still had not returned so they all went inside while Promise packed up her and Zaire's things. She didn't want any of the furniture or electronics besides her laptop. She just packed up her wardrobe, jewelry, cosmetics, some linen, Zaire's clothes and two boxes full of his toys.

Antiwan loaded up all of her luggage on the bed of his Ford F-150. Then they all left before Murda returned.

Promise rode shotgun with Antiwan while Xena and Zaire rode in her BMW because Xena and Antiwan both had military I.D.'s. Their house on the base was only a two bedroom so they gave Promise and Zaire their sons' room, temporarily. The boys would have to sleep on the couch's pull-out bed in the den. Promise was embarrassed and she promised Xena that she wouldn't be there for more than a couple of weeks. Xena just gave her a warm embrace, then assured her that she could stay for as long as she needed to, free of charge.

❖ ❖

Murda returned to his crib in Annapolis later on that Friday afternoon, after Winter told him that she didn't want anything else to do with him. She never told him why they were separating, but he could tell that she meant business from the iciness in her tone. That's when he decided to give her some time and space to cool down, and go home to his other babymama, Promise. He was dumbfounded when he walked into the house, seeing that the entire living room had been ransacked. He immediately noticed all of the missing electronics and automatically concluded that a robbery had occurred. That's when he pulled his all-black 40-cal from his waistband and cocked it back. Then he yelled out to Promise and Zaire, racing up the stairs.

Murda really started to panic when he noticed the droplets of blood on the stairs and the bullet-hole in the wall. First he checked Zaire's room, and then he went into their bedroom. When he didn't find them, and noticed all of the opened drawers, he was baffled. "Why the hell would the robbers steal all of Promise's and Zaire's clothes? They must've been crack heads", he thought.

Murda dialed Promise's cell number several times but she avoided his calls each time. He didn't know if she and Zaire had been kidnapped, bodied or what. He didn't know what to do, but calling the cops would definitely be his last resort. He became even more perplexed when he noticed that the safe in his closet was untouched. That's where some of his cash was, at least 50 grand.

Murda went frantic. He called up a bunch of his blood homies and they all rushed over for a meeting, what they called a "Nine". Over twenty Bloods arrived in less than a half hour. They all filtered into the house one by one, all strapped and ready to hold court in the streets. All Murda had to do was give the word. None of his bloods had a clue about where Promise was, or who had broken into his crib. For almost 45 minutes, they all made calls to see if anyone had heard anything. Then they all hopped in their rides and spread out all over the city, in hopes that they might spot Promise's BMW somewhere. Her customized cherry-red paint job made it easy to spot her from a mile away.

That day, Murda and his goons had no luck in finding Promise. He spent the following week almost worrying himself bald. Both Promise and Winter were ducking his calls and, now all of a sudden, he began realizing that Promise was the best thing that had ever happened to him. Everything seemed to be falling apart, like the domino effect. Being without her enabled him to think about his life more lucidly. His crack spot in Cherry Hill got rushed by the feds that week, leaving him with even more bond money to kick out for seven more of his workers. He was so distraught that he started to really let himself go, smoking dippers day and night. *I guess that's the way that the cookie crumbles when you shit on people who love you.*

Before he knew it, three weeks had passed and he still hadn't heard a word from Promise. Meanwhile, she was doing just fine.

Antiwan had hooked her up with a half-ass job, working as a cashier at the Commissary on base. She was only two paychecks away from paying the security deposit and first month's rent for a two-bedroom flat that she had found out in Bowie, Maryland. Murda was miserable, and he'd been sleeping alone at the crib in Annapolis almost every night. Then one night, while he was asleep, he heard his doorbell ring. Awakened by the sound, he glanced at his digital alarm clock on the nightstand and noticed that it was 3:17 a.m.

Murda just knew that couldn't have been anyone but Promise and Zaire, finally set free by their captors. He hurried downstairs to the front door, dressed in some basketball shorts and a black t-shirt emblazoned with Tony Montana's image on the front. He quickly opened the door without thinking twice about who was on the other side of it. When he opened it, to his surprise, he was met by two white fed agents dressed in civilian clothes. Behind them, was a black unmarked Crown Victoria parked in the driveway.

"Joseph Reed?" asked the shorter one.

Murda's heart started to thud, afraid that he was about to learn that Promise and Zaire's bodies were found slain somewhere. He answered, "I'm Joseph".

Then the taller officer ordered, "Turn around and put your hands behind your back, you're under arrest".

"Why?" Murda countered.

Then, without answering his question, the officer continued, "You have the right to remain silent. Anything that you say can and will be used against you in the court of law. You have the right to an attorney, and if you cant afford...."

"I know my fuckin Miranda rights," Murda retorted.

"Why am I being arrested?" he continued, as he turned around to be handcuffed.

Those wicked-ass cops hauled Murda off to jail while he was still barefooted and everything. When he realized that he was being taken to Baltimore, he asked again, "Why am I going to jail?"

The driver finally gave him an answer, "Dope! You sold to one of our informants this weekend and now its time to pay the piper."

Murda knew that was some bullshit because he never made any sales hand to hand. He had runners to do that shit for him. Now feeling like their case against him was frivolous, he started taunting them. "You can't book me Danno. I'll be out faster than you can blink. Plus I've got lawyers that'll eat this case alive".

The officer in the passenger's seat laughed at his presumption, as if to say, "Sure, and my name's Mickey Mouse."

Murda sat in the back seat, staring out of the window at the skyline as they crossed over the bridge that brings you into downtown Baltimore. Then he looked to the sky to see if there was a black cloud following him. He wondered who had set him up, where Promise was, and how long it would be before he would see that beautiful skyline once again.

When the officers escorted Murda into the jail, they had him booked in, then placed him in a holding tank with ten other men who were arrested that same night. The booking officer gave Murda a pair of black and white shower-shoes to put on. In the holding tank, all of the other men were trading stories about how and why they got arrested. Murda wasn't pressed for none of that shit. He just wanted to make a phone call to his lawyer and appear before the judge for a bond hearing. It was almost 6:00 a.m. when Murda was finally given a 15-minute collect call so that he could call his lawyer, Mark Nettles. His firm didn't open until 9:00 so Murda tried his cell. When Nettles heard Murda's name in the recording, he quickly accepted.

"Mr. Reed?" he asked.

Murda answered, "Yeah Mark, listen. Somebody set me up. These fuckin' alphabet boys are saying that I sold to an informant this weekend, but I was home all weekend".

Nettles knew that Murda was very organized and that he couldn't have possibly made a careless mistake like that. He also knew how slimy the feds were and the measures that they would take to try and make the charges stick.

Mr. Nettles asked Murda, "Do you have any witnesses who can attest to the fact that you were home all weekend, like your girl?"

He replied, "No, she disappeared on me. I was ducked-off in the crib like a hermit for almost two weeks, going through some things".

"Well, what time is your bond hearing? I'll try to shoot up there and talk to the judge. I may know him and I'll try to convince him to give you a reasonable bond."

"You need to be here by 7:30", Murda replied. Then they ended the call so that he could get dressed and hurry down to the jail.

Around 8:15, Murda and five other men were escorted to a small courtroom, shackled by the ankles with their hands cuffed in front of them. He immediately noticed Mr. Nettles waiting in the courtroom, wearing an all-gray Giorgio Armani single-breasted suit with a white button-up and a gray necktie. He told Murda that he didn't know that judge personally because he was a circuit judge from another city. The judge told Mr. Nettles that he was gonna have to deny Murda's bond, due to the amount of coke that he was being charged with. His indictment papers stated that he had sold exactly 1,008 grams of coke to an informant, an entire key.

Murda couldn't believe this shit, it seemed surreal. His bond was denied while the other four guys all got released on their own recognizance. They had misdemeanor charges like public drunk and hopping the Light Rail. Murda and the other men were escorted back to the holding tank, immediately after they appeared before the judge. Murda had to wait to be dressed-out and assigned to a pod, while the others were waiting to be processed-out and released. Murda couldn't wait to be moved to a pod so that he could leave that filthy ass holding tank, reeked with a putrid smell like piss. Plus there were green and yellow-ish stains all over the floor and the walls, some of which were probably old dried-up semen stains. He knew that, whatever pod he moved into, he would have blood homies there because they flooded the jail and his name rung bells.

It was almost noon when Murda finally got dressed-out. Before he was given a shower, a tall white male officer told him to strip completely naked so that he could be sprayed down with this spray that was supposed to kill crabs and lice. The officer stood a few feet away and asked Murda to raise both arms so that he could spray his arm pits. Then he made him lift his dick and sprayed his balls. Next, the officer told him to turn around and he sprayed his ass and the back of his legs. Murda felt violated like a muthafucka, plus the spray was brick-cold. Then he was allowed to take a 5 minute shower that was even colder. He held his breath and cringed every muscle in his body to fight against the ice-cold water that streamed all over him. He just wanted to wash off the stench of that funky-ass holding tank.

Murda was dressed-out in an inmate jumpsuit. Then he was escorted down a long hallway to his pod. When he entered his pod, the entire top tier was out for rec. Men were playing cards, playing chess, watching tv, talking on the payphones, and taking showers. Murda walked over to the officer's desk to find out what cell he was assigned to. Suddenly, he began hearing several of the inmates in the pod yelling out different blood calls. "Bddddattt, Bddddattt!", "Suuuwuuu!" Murda received his room assignment then walked towards the circle of bloods.

Halfway there, one of them approached Murda and asked, "What's poppin' blood?" Murda answered, "You already know, five poppin' and six droppin'", as they began doing a blood handshake. He didn't have enough time to dap everyone of them because the officer rushed him to his cell, threatening to send him to a maximum security unit if he didn't go into his cell immediately. His cell was located on the bottom tier which had already been out for rec earlier. As he carried his things to his cell, his blood homies continued to salute him, making more blood calls, "Big B's homie!" "B's up!", Murda replied, while throwing up a blood sign with his right hand.

6

WHEN THE TABLES TURN

Murda was fortunate enough to have a one-man cell. He spent that first night lying on his rack, staring at the ceiling, and wondering who had set him up. "Could it had been Cool, Redrum or Bang Bang? Or could it be those three crack head bitches, who knows?" he thought. He considered the fact that 7 of his other workers got hemmed up during the Cherry Hill raid. It could've been anybody. He was hoping that either Cool, Redrum or Bang Bang was on his rotation when the bottom tier came out for rec the next morning. He wanted some answers. He didn't know if one of them was in the pod or not. All he knew was that they were all separated from each other because Cool's girl had told him that. After realizing that he couldn't possibly figure the shit out, he began thinking of questions to ask his lawyer on the next morning when he called.

Murda didn't get a wink of sleep that night; thoughts bouncing back and forth from Promise, to Zaire, to his fucked up predicament. He didn't have an appetite the next morning when the C.O. delivered his breakfast tray, but he was waiting at the door when he came to let him out for rec at 7:30. That's when he walked towards the payphone, doing the knowledge to his surroundings. He was looking around to see if he would spot any of his old enemies or one of his workers. Murda wasn't shook at all, and he was definitely down to squabble with any nigga that wanted to try him.

When Murda didn't recognize any of the other inmates, he proceeded with his call to his lawyer. Mr. Nettles said that the feds weren't going to ease up and that he could forget about getting a bond. Right now, he was looking like Public Enemy #one. When Murda asked how long he would have to sit, Nettles said that depended on rather he wanted to plead guilty or not. If he decided to plead guilty, he could be sentenced and shipped in no time. But, if he wanted to take his shit to trial, it could take forever. Plus he would be facing the maximum.

Murda argued, "Plead to what?! These fuckin' burgers don't have shit on me!"

Then Mr. Nettles interjected, "Here's the deal. I spoke to the DEA. They said that they have your voice on tape making a drug transaction. They wouldn't have taken things this far if they didn't have strong evidence against you."

Murda spat, "Who the fuck did I sell to?"

Mr. Nettles gave a deep sigh, then answered, "Here's the thing...you do have the right to cross-examine your witnesses but only in the event of a trial. When you plead guilty, you waive that right. The feds are willing to offer you ten years if you plead, but if you try to take this to trial, you'll risk the possibility of receiving an L-Wop."

Murda furrowed his eyebrows and asked, "What the hell is an L-Wop?"

"Life without parole", Nettles replied flatly.

Murda wanted to reach through the phone and punch him right in his snot box. That's when he barked on him, "What the fuck am i paying you for? You're already like 100 grand in the red with me. Don't have me to send my soldiers your way. You know they'll plant your stupid ass!"

Mr. Nettles knew that the bloods were a force to be reckoned with. He didn't really know what to say because he knew deep down that his hands were tied. That's when he just blurted out, "Just take it easy. Give me a few days to work my magic and I'll be down there to visit you soon". Realizing that he was only trying to buy time, Murda hung up in his face. He tried to call Promise next but her phone just rang until the voicemail greeting came on.

❖ ❖

Promise had no idea that Murda had been arrested. She rarely even left the base because she was being very frugal, trying to save every penny that she had towards her crib. Her days were spent working and her nights were spent taking care of Zaire. Xena didn't have a job so she would babysit for her until she knocked off every evening around 5:00. Whenever Zaire would fall asleep at night, Promise would work on her book for hours until she too would eventually doze off.

Antiwan spoke to his superiors about Promise's situation and got her hooked up with an employee pass that would enable her to enter the military base everyday after she moved out to Bowie. Her book was almost completed and she had begun searching for different publishers online, to submit her manuscript to. She emailed her first six chapters to ten different publishers, along with a cover letter, but none of them got back with her. Still, she never got discouraged. She refused to give up like her mother did.

Xena couldn't stand to see how depressed Promise always looked, moping around for weeks on end. She barely even came out of the bedroom, always planted in front of that damn laptop. She could tell that, deep down, she was missing Murda. She only had one week left before time to move into her own crib, and Xena wanted to have at least one more girls' night out with her. She wanted to cheer her up because she knew that Promise was getting weak, and probably ready to forgive Murda and take him back. Xena walked into Promise's room around 7:00 that Friday night, and said,

"Alright girl, you've been moping around in here for almost a month now. We don't even talk like we used to and you're living under the same roof now. I already know that you're still hung up over Murda, let it go already."

Promise replied, "Xena, I can't lie. I miss being a family. I know he wasn't perfect but every relationship has it's ups and downs".

Xena wasn't hearing that shit. That's when she said, sternly, "No, Promise. You have to get over that nigga. Sometimes I really think you need a check-up from the neck up. He put his hands on you, he never stayed home, plus the nigga has a whole nother family...with a white bitch at that. You need to just put on your fuck 'em dress, do something to that nappy-ass head of yours, and let's go out. My treat."

"Go where?" Promise asked.

"I don't know, let's just go out to dinner, and then we can hit the club."

"Why, so I can run into Murda or one of his blood homies?"

Xena laughed and continued, "I aint talking about no kiddies' club like Hammerjacks or the Paradox. As a matter of fact, we can just drive out to D.C. I know an upscale club called the K Street Lounge on U Street, like three blocks away from Adams Morgan."

Promise took a long and deep breath, and then she murmured, "I don't know, Xena."

Xena said, "Look Promise, you're too beautiful to be stressing over that ugly-ass nigga. My mother always told me that the best way to get over one man is to get under another one."

They both started laughing together, and then Promise finally agreed. "Okay Xena, give me an hour and a half to get dressed."

Promise sifted through her entire wardrobe, trying to decide on an outfit to wear. She decided to throw on this red silk BCBG mini dress and a pair of red satin pumps made by Sergio Rossi. Then she took a hot shower for almost 30 minutes. She flat-ironed her hair, put on a little bit of eye shadow and some lip gloss. Then she put on her dress and her pumps. She then put on her diamond encrusted Chanel earrings with a red Chanel purse to match her dress. To top it all off, she snapped on her gold Cartier watch and put on a pair of Roberto Cavalli sunglasses with red frames. That night she looked jaw-dropping and she knew it.

Xena knocked on the door around 9:00 to see if she was dressed yet, and Promise invited her in. When Xena noticed how stunning she looked, she said, "Now that's my bestie! That's the Promise that I remember". Xena was looking good too. She was rocking a blue and gray spaghetti strapped Christian Dior dress and some blue and gray heels made by Michael Kors. Plus she had the blue and gray YSL Handbag to match.

They hopped in Promise's BMW looking like two NBA housewives. Antiwan had agreed to watch the boys. The girls' first stop was at this restaurant in Landover called Stonefish Bar and Grill. They wanted to put some food in their stomachs because they both had decided to get ripped that night. When they arrived at the K Street Lounge, they noticed that the line was wrapped around the building. Promise parallel parked her car on U Street, not far from the club. They walked past the general admissions line and headed straight for the V.I.P. entrance. They knew that they were both too fine that night to be waiting in that long-ass line. Xena gave the security guard a crispy $100 bill and he removed the red velvet rope that was blocking the V.I.P. entrance.

When they walked into the club, Promise immediately noticed how plush the club was. The setting was on some real grown and sexy shit. No white Tees, jeans or sneakers. All of the guys were dressed casually, rocking hard-bottoms or loafers. The other women in the room didn't have anything on Promise or Xena. There were some gorgeous women, true enough. But, Promise and Xena were the pick of the litter, hands down. Xena and Promise found a vacant table and flagged down a waitress to order some drinks. Xena ordered some Moscato and Promise ordered some Absolut with cranberry juice.

Promise was definitely loving the scenery and the attention. The one thing that she wasn't feeling was the music. You know DC niggas be on that go-go shit. She was more into house music, what they always played in Baltimore clubs. Most of the men seemed too intimidated to approach their table, even though Promise saw a few who appealed to her. She just wasn't about to make the first move. Xena was only there to show Promise a good time. She was happily married and satisfied with her man at home.

The girls were laughing and joking at their table when a waitress delivered a bucket of ice to their table with two bottles of Moet Gold Label. That's when Promise stuck out her hand and said, "Wrong table hun, we didn't order these." The woman laughed and replied, "I know ma'am, these are courtesy of that gentleman over there," pointing to a table behind them. When they both looked back, they saw a tall and muscular brown-skinned man sitting at a table by himself. Xena whispered, "Damn he's fine", through clenched teeth. Promise concurred. That's when they both waved and Promise smiled at him, showing her perfect white teeth. Then the waitress continued, "And he also told me to give you this". That's when she handed a small business card to Promise and headed back towards the mini-bar to fill another order.

When Promise looked at the card, the name read Andre Vasquez, CEO/Chairman of True Life Publishing. Xena told Promise, "That nigga must like you for real...sending us two bottles of Mo. At least go over and say thank you". Promise was acting all coy while Xena played her alter ego, like the devil on her left shoulder. "Just look at that sexy-ass nigga, he looks ten times better than Murda. If it was me, and I wasn't married, I'd be all over his ass."

The alcohol was beginning to take its effect and, after a few more sips, Promise finally found the courage to walk over to his table alone. Xena remained at their table, taking periodic sips of Moet and texting Antiwan. A few guys tried to approach her but she just flashed the huge diamond on her wedding ring and gracefully turned them away.

The man spotted Promise walking towards his table so he stood up. Then she reached out her hand and introduced herself, "Hi, I'm Promise". He replied, "Dre". When he spoke, his deep baritone voice sent a chill all the way down her spine. As he kissed the back of her hand, Promise sized him up from head to toe. He was rocking a low caesar with a bee hive and long sideburns. He had on an all-black Gucci suit with a gray and black Gucci neck-tie, a white button-up, and a pair of all-black Gucci loafers. At first touch, she noticed his big-strong hands. Plus she could tell that he was kinda brolic underneath that suit.

They sat next to each other and started chopping it up. Dre said that he was originally from Southeast Washington D.C., and that he grew up on Alabama Avenue. He was divorced with two daughters. He admitted that he was an ex-drug dealer, plus an ex-con, but he went legit and currently owned a publishing company that was doing a lot of numbers. He had approximately fifteen authors under his imprint and his company had released over fifty titles already.

As he was telling his story, Promise was admiring everything about him, his eyes, his lips, his teeth, and also his rich DC accent. In the back of her mind, she began telling herself, "I'm gonna fuck this nigga tonight". From the look in his eyes, she knew for certain that he wanted the same thing. She knew that she was sexually frustrated, and that she just needed to bust a couple of nuts with no strings attached. "And who better than this prince charming-ass nigga for the job?" she thought. She didn't know this dude from Adam. She was feeling tipsy, Dre was saying all of the right things, and Promise's pussy was thumping at 100 miles per hour.

Dre took a sip of his Ciroc just as the dj was switching songs. That's when Promise laughed and said, "This is probably the only go-go song that I like". It was Sexy Lady by the UCB Band. Dre realized what she was insinuating so he grabbed her by the hand and escorted her to the dance floor. As they were walking, Promise winked at Xena, smiling devilishly. Xena winked back and gave her two thumbs up. Dre and Promise walked to a spot on the dance floor that was well-lit and not too crowded.

All of that shy shit went out the window. They started out dancing really close, face to face. Then Promise turned around and pressed her round ass up against his dick. She could feel that he was rock-hard and she was soaking wet. She hadn't felt that free in a long time. She closed her eyes, bit down on her bottom lip, and grabbed his neck-tie; pulling him closer to her face. He placed both hands on her waist. As she was backing it up on him, her mini dress raised up and she could feel his hardness rubbing up against her wetness. She was about to lose control, and that's when she whispered into his ear, "Can I go home with you?" Without hesitation, he answered, "Hell yeah ma, lets blow this joint."

They left the dance floor and walked over to Xena's table. Promise asked Xena, "Can you take my car home and pick me up in the morning? I'm about to go out to eat with my new friend". They had already eaten before going to the club so Xena knew what time it was. Even though she felt like it was kinda promiscuous for Promise to fuck Dre so soon, she wasn't gonna try to dissuade her this time. She probably wanted Promise to do it more than she did, all so she could get over Murda. She despised his ass.

When Xena agreed, Promise grabbed the unopened bottle of Moet and they all exited the club together. When they walked outside, Xena hopped in the Beamer and Promise followed Dre to his silver and red Lamborghini Sesto Elemento. It was roughly 2:00 a.m. They drove out to his 2-story brick house on Pennsylvania Avenue. As soon as they stepped out of the car, Promise popped the cork on the Moet and started drinking straight from the bottle. She was acting kinda wild and staggering a little bit as they made their way up the steps.

As soon as Dre closed the door, Promise was all over him, tonguing him down. He practically ripped his shirt off, then grabbed her by the ass and lifted her up. She wrapped her legs around his waist and they kissed all the way to his bedroom. Dre laid her down on his king-sized canopy bed and she came out of her dress. They never even turned the lights on.

Promise was looking so beautiful that he couldn't resist kissing her entire body, then going down and licking her pussy.

She spread both legs with her feet planted flat on the bed, and let Dre go to work on her. She let herself get all the way into it because she was horny as fuck and she hadn't had any dick since Murda, almost two months earlier. Dre ate her pussy like it was the last supper. His heavy tongue kept her sugar walls coming down and she busted three nuts back to back. It felt so good that she wanted to suck his dick. When he saw how wet she was, he strapped on a Magnum, and thrust himself inside of her.

In the silence of the room, the only sound was the smacking sound of their lips kissing each other. As Dre stroked her missionary style, her pussy was also making a smacking sound because it was so wet. Promise grabbed his ass and pulled him deeper and deeper inside of her. When he began sweating, she wiped the sweat beads from his forehead with her hand as she begged him not to stop. They went for hours and Dre put it down better than Murda ever did. Then they slept naked with each other until the morning came.

7

HIT AND RUN

Promise woke up around 8:30 that morning. Dre was still out for the count so she just laid there and admired his chiseled-up body. He had a couple of tats and he also had surgery scars on his stomach, probably where a bullet had been removed. Promise couldn't believe that she had just had a one-night stand with this perfect stranger, neither could she believe how good it was. She and Murda had never made love so passionately, and the memories of last night were tempting her to ask for another round.

The alcohol had worn off, and she didn't have that aggressiveness anymore. She was actually type-embarrassed, considering what Dre probably thought of her for opening her legs on the first night. That's when Promise grabbed her cell phone and texted Xena, telling her to pick her up at his address. Xena texted back in a matter of seconds saying that she was on her way.

Promise climbed out of the bed and grabbed her dress and her panties off the floor. Then she got dressed while Dre remained asleep. She sat quietly in a chair by the bedroom-window, looking through the blinds and waiting for Xena to pull up out front. When Xena arrived almost half an hour later, Dre was still in La La Land. Those few nuts must've really drained him. She grabbed her purse and walked out without even waking him up to say goodbye. As she and Xena drove off, she looked back through her rearview mirror to see if Dre would ever come out. He never did.

"So, what happened girl? I wanna know every intricate detail," said Xena, barely keeping her eyes on the road.

Promise reclined her seat back, chuckled and said, "Nothing happened, stop being nosy".

Then she turned to face the window, avoiding eye contact. "Wake me up when we get home", said Promise as she pretended to be going to sleep.

Knowing that Promise was probably exhausted from getting her back blown out all night, she left her alone for a few minutes. Curiosity was killing the cat and, before long, she was at it again.

"Promise, you've gotta fill me in." "Alright Xena damn. We fucked, alright?", Promise replied.

Xena laughed and said, "Duh...I figured that much. How was it?"

Promise hesitated until she couldn't hold it in any longer. "Oh my God Xena, that shit felt so good. That nigga knows he can eat a pussy too!" Promise was making herself horny just thinking about it.

That's when Xena glared into her eyes and asked, "You sucked his dick too, didn't you?"

Promise held her stare and sneered, "Hell no! Don't try to carry me Xena." "I'm just joanin on you girl. I'm just glad that it was him instead of that bamma-ass Murda."

When they arrived at Xena's house almost 20 minutes later, Promise went straight to bed and slept until around noon. That's when she was awakened by her cell phone ringing. She had avoided every call that morning but someone seemed to be calling back to back. When she looked at her caller I.D., it was a 1-877 number. She assumed that it was probably some annoying bill collector or some telemarketer trying to sell something. After pressing the ignore button, she realized that they had already called four times that morning.

The phone rang a few seconds later and she answered it immediately. "Hello!"

After a few seconds of silence from the other end, she repeated herself a little bit louder. Then a recording began,

"Hello, you have a collect call from 'Murda' in the Baltimore City Jail. To accept the charges for this call, press zero. If you wish not to accept this call, please hang up now."

Promise hesitated to accept the call, wondering what he could've possibly been arrested for. Then she finally pressed zero and the recording continued, "Go ahead with your call."

"Promise?" Murda asked.

"Yeah Murda", she snarled, releasing a deep sigh.

"Damn Promise, where have you been all this time? You had me worried sick."

"Zaire and I have been fine", she answered.

First, she explained the burglary incident to him. Then she finally fessed up to meeting Winter and knowing about his other two sons. That's when he realized why both women had been acting so cold towards him. Realizing that he was busted, he never denied the accusations. He apologized instead, making claims that he had changed.

Promise realized what direction the conversation was going in, so she interjected, "And why are you in jail again?"

He replied, "I got set up bay. The feds picked me up on a bogus coke charge, but enough about me. Where are you sleeping at night, in a hotel?"

"I've been staying with Xena. I'm getting my own crib next week."

"With what?"

"I have a job now."

Murda barked, "Promise, you don't have to work for nobody. And besides, it's only been a month so you can't have that much money saved up. Where are you moving to, the projects?" She replied, "I found a crib out in Bowie. It's in a good neighborhood. I'll just have to wait a few weeks before I can rent some furniture."

Murda became furious at the thought of Promise and Zaire sleeping in an unfurnished house. That's when he said, "I have at least 50 grand in my safe. Call Bloodbath and have him to go back to the house with you. Take $20,000 for your furniture and hold the other 30 thousand until I tell you to give it to my lawyer".

Promise declined, "Murda, I don't want your money". He insisted, "I know but take it anyway. We can't have Za Za sleeping on the floor, right?"

As much as Promise wanted to refuse the cash, she knew deep down that she really needed it. She also knew that if she accepted it, she would be allowing Murda to come back into the picture. She pondered for a few moments until she overheard the c.o. yell out that Rec would be over in five minutes. That's when Murda told her to grab an ink pen. When she returned to the phone with a pen and pad in hand, he continued, "Write down 34-22-18". After she wrote down the digits, she asked, "Whats that?" "The combination to the safe", he replied.

Murda hung up the phone, feeling relieved that he had finally talked to Promise. He had planned to call again on the next day. When he returned to his cell, he wrote out three kites. One was for Cool, another for Bang Bang, and the last one was for Redrum. He had met another blood named Bloodsport. He was a trustee who had free run of the facility. He could move throughout the jail with very little risk of being frisked or searched. He didn't know Cool, Redrum, or Bang Bang but he assured Murda that he could find them. He told Murda to have the kites ready by 5:00 that evening, when he and two other trustees would deliver the dinner trays to his pod. Murda took down his name and inmate I.D. number so that he could put $100 on his books for delivering the kites for him.

In each kite, Murda explained that he had been set up and that his lawyer was still working on getting their bonds set. Around 3:00 that afternoon, all of the inmates were in their cells and Murda was taking a power nap. That's when the dorm officer's voice came yelling through the small intercom in his cell. "Mr. Reed, get dressed. You have a visit." Murda knew that regular visitation hours were from 6 p.m. to 9 p.m. so he figured that Mark, his lawyer, had finally come to deliver some good news. He was so curious that he didn't even waste time on washing his face or brushing his teeth. He just squeezed some toothpaste onto his tongue. Then he pressed the "TALK" button on the intercom and said, "I'm ready, pop my door".

The officer in the control booth pressed a button on the control panel and caused Murda's cell door to slide open, then he walked out into the empty pod. A different officer was waiting to escort him down the hall to receive his visit. Instead of going to the visitation room, he was taken to an interrogation room. And, instead of finding his attorney, he found two fed agents and a black and gray Sony tape recorder. Murda was told to have a seat as he wondered what these men had up their sleeves. One agent was this tall, slender built, dark-skinned cat. He didn't have the police-look at all. The nigga had braids, plus he was wearing jeans and a white-t.

He began, "So, Mr. Reed, we hope that you understand that these are very serious charges that we have against you. You could receive natural life without parole. We may be able to work things out where you can get off on an acquittal. You know...you look out for us, and we'll look out for you". Murda threw on his poker face as if he wasn't gonna budge. Then he mustered the balls to say, "I aint no snitch. I love the streets and the streets love me". The other agent, this tall and muscular white guy, banged his fist on the table and threatened, "Look, you fuckin' prick, don't give us that shit. We're trying to give you a break here. You fuck with us and you're gonna fall like the London Bridge. We could've confiscated all those nice cars, that house and everything else. Plus we could arrest that Promise chick since almost everything is in her name. You just think about that tough guy!"

The agent recognized that he had just penetrated a sensitive spot in Murda's mind so he calmly passed him his card and suggested, "Just think about it". Murda was then escorted back to his cell, now feeling like he was really having a meltdown. He couldn't wait until evening Rec at 7:30, when he could give his lawyer a call. He passed the kites off to Bloodsport at dinner time and waited patiently in his cell until Rec time.

When the officer opened his cell at 7:30, he walked straight to the payphone and dialed Mr. Nettles' cell number. As soon as he accepted the call, Murda began chewing his ears off.

"Yo Mark, you'd better have some fuckin' good news for me!"

Mark was nervous as hell, trying to be careful not to piss him off any further. He took a deep exhale and said, "Mr. Reed, I'm doing everything within my powers. I requested your motion of discovery and I'm gonna review all of their evidence before I decide on how we're gonna attack this. I'm just waiting to get my hands on that tape".

Murda spat, "But, I thought that a tape wasn't admissible in court. This is some real bullshit Mark!"

"The feds can practically do whatever they wanna do. You know that."

"Fuck that! If you don't get me out of here soon, you're gonna be swimming with the fishes. I go up for another bond hearing after 90 days. I'm gonna give you another 30 grand and you'd better make something shake with that!"

Mr. Nettles knew that there was really nothing that he could do. He also knew that if he refused the cash, Murda would realize that and have him murdered in no time. He just remained silent until Murda spoke his piece, then he agreed to visit him on the following day. When Murda hung up the phone, he was so vexed that his blood was bubbling in his veins. He was going through withdrawals from the dippers, plus his whole world seemed discombobulated.

Rec wasn't over until 8:30 so Murda decided to take a hot shower. Afterwards, he was gonna call Promise to warn her not to go back to the house because of what the feds had told him. When he stepped out of the shower, he had approximately twenty minutes left. That's when he posted up by the payphones and waited for a phone to become available.

This one guy with dreads had been using one of the phones ever since Murda had called his lawyer. There were three other guys using phones but they had all just sat down in the last 5 minutes. Murda knew that each call only lasted for 15 minutes so he told the dread-head that he needed to use that particular phone when he was done talking. The guy looked back at Murda, distastefully, as if to say, "Picture that shit". Then Murda folded his arms and played the wall until the duration of his call. When he looked up at the clock again, it was 8:20. He could hear that the guy was ending his call so he moved in closer. The man hung up the phone but remained seated like he was thinking of some random person to call out of spite. Then he put the phone back to his ear and began dialing a new number.

Murda walked over to the man and argued, "Aye homie...I need to use the horn. We only have ten minutes left and you've been riding all night". The dread-head screwed up his face, looked back once again, and said, "Nigga you'll use the phone when I'm done". Then he turned around to continue with his call. The person on the other end must've asked him who he was talking to because he answered, "Some slob-ass nigga". Right then, Murda dropped his shower bag and punched the guy in his face, knocking him out of his chair. Then he commenced to stomping him out on the floor.

The other inmates in the pod rushed over to watch the fight, some of them clutching like they were carrying knives. Then, the two dorm officers rushed to the scene, panicking and calling for back-up on their walkie-talkie radios. They demanded that all of the other inmates moved back as a group of sergeants and lieutenants filtered in from both of the exit doors. That's when most of the inmates cleared the space. By then, Murda had straddled the man's chest and was feeding him blow after blow to the face. Both dorm officers drew a can of pepper spray from their holsters and began spraying both men in their faces.

The other inmates scattered like roaches as the gas began to spread throughout the pod. The two lieutenants grabbed each one of them and broke up the fight. The dread-head was stunned, almost unconscious. Murda was holding his eyes shut tightly, yelling because they were burning from the pepper spray. Everybody was coughing and sneezing. The other inmates were ordered to stand in front of their cells while Murda and the other guy were handcuffed and taken out of the pod.

Murda's knuckles were bloody and the other guy was all lumped up. Murda had definitely represented for the bloods in his pod and made an example out of him. On the way out, neither one of them could hardly breathe. They were both taken to the nurse to have their eyes cleaned with cold water. Then they were given cold showers. The pepper spray burned their skin even worse when the water hit it. When they were done, they were both taken to the Maximum Security Unit. Once in the MSU, they were both stripped down to their boxers, then thrown into one-man cells. When Murda walked into his cell, the first thing that he noticed was the filth. There was a stone slab along the wall, apparently where he was supposed to sleep at because there was no mattress in sight. There was a dirty toilet, but there was no tissue in the room. And, the room was freezing. There was a vent below the sink and the a/c was on full-blast. He could literally see the cold air as it whistled through the vent. Murda started kicking on the door, trying to get the c.o.'s attention. The lieutenant had left the wing but there was an officer behind the glass in the officers' station, located in the center of the unit.

Murda kicked and banged on the door for over thirty minutes until he heard another man's voice coming from the opposite side of the vent. The man's voice was saying, "Aye next door...next door". The way that he rolled his r's, Murda assumed that he must've been a Puerto Rican.

When Murda realized that the man was referring to him, he answered, "What the fuck do you want young?"

"I just wanted to let you know that you're wasting your time kicking on that door. These pigs don't give a fuck about us."

That's when Murda asked, "Do you have a mattress over there?"

The man replied, "Yeah, you will get a mat, a jumpsuit and some toilet-paper some time tomorrow. They're gonna make you suffer tonight though. That's how they do everybody".

Murda didn't say anything else to his vent-partner that night. Instead, he curled up on the stone slab in attempts to keep warm and fall asleep. For Murda, that was the longest night ever. The guy that he was fighting with was a few cells down, frequently making threats on the door throughout the night. When the officer brought Murda's breakfast around 6:30 the next morning, he had only managed to get about thirty minutes of sleep. He was disgusted when he realized that he was being served what they called nutraloaf. It was cold grits, bits of eggs, sausage and bread compressed into a loaf. He didn't eat it immediately, but he didn't throw it away either because he knew that he would soon be hungry.

The MSU officer brought Murda a mat, a blanket, a jumpsuit, and a roll of tissue around 11:30 that morning. Murda got dressed with the quickness as he asked the officer when he was gonna be given a phone call. The officer laughed at him and replied, "Not on my shift". He was a little faggot-ass light skinned dude, real feminine, plus he spoke with a lisp. Murda's room was still freezing so he used most of his tissue to cover the holes on the vent. He had to wet the tissue first. Then the cold air caused it to dry up like plaster over the vent.

8

THE PLOT THICKENS

Promise stayed in the crib all day long on Sunday, spending quality time with Zaire and working on her book. She was only three chapters away from the ending. She just relaxed for the majority of that evening because she had a busy work-week ahead of her. She had planned to move into her new home on Friday, as soon as she knocked off from her job. Meanwhile, Murda was raising hell all day long in his cell. He was on fire because he wasn't given a phone call or a shower, plus he was served nutra loaf for all three meals that day.

Around 7:30 that evening, when the sun set, Murda's next-door neighbor spoke through the vent once again. This time, his voice sounded muffled because of the tissue that was covering the vent. He was saying, "Aye next door".

Murda peeled back some of the tissue so that he could hear him better. Then he answered, "Yeah, what's up mo?"

"Yo, I'm gonna get the C.O. to pass you a few of these XXL magazines in the morning. I know that you're bored as hell over there."

Murda replied, "That's what it is homie".

"My name is Joe by the way, what they call you fam?"

"They call me Bloody Murda."

"Oh you're Blood?" the man asked.

Then Murda replied, "All the time".

The man asked Murda what he had done to be sent to the MSU. Murda told him about the fight, and then he asked him the exact same question. That's when the man said that he was placed in the MSU for protective custody. Without shame, he admitted that he had testified against some cat from West Baltimore and that he didn't feel safe in general population. He was allowed to check-in on PC until he was processed out and released in the next couple of days.

When Murda realized that he was talking to a snitch, he gracefully fell back from the vent. Then he laid back on his mat and stared up at the ceiling until around 10:00. That's when Joe got back on the vent, pressed for rap.

"Aye Bloody Murda."

Murda answered, "Yeah".

"How long have you been banging blood?"

Murda snapped, "Look bro, I don't know what you're talking about", paranoid that Joe was fishing for information to write in his next statement.

Joe peeped the play and said, "Man, I know you're thinking I'm some rat trying to set you up. But, you don't have to worry about that. I was only asking because my last roommate was a blood and we used to talk about that shit".

Murda was really strict about Blood knowledge being shared with off-brands so he was curious to know what Joe's old roommate had revealed to him. Thats when he asked, "Oh yeah?"

Joe answered, "Yeah, his name was Bang Bang".

Right then, it was like a light bulb had popped up in Murda's head. Then he asked, "Oh word? What pod is he in?"

Without hesitation, Joe replied, "That nigga went home already. He left about a week ago".

At that moment, Bang Bang became Murda's primary suspect. He knew that the feds only gave bonds to snitches or people who were willing to set niggas up.

Murda asked, "So, is he out on bond or did he get time-served?"

Joe replied, "I don't mean any disrespect because I know that snitching goes against the bloods' protocol, but Bang Bang is working for the Feds. They let him walk because he agreed to set up this big-time weight man out in Annapolis".

Certain that this man wasn't making this up, Murda leaned closer towards the vent and asked, "So he told you that?"

Full of zeal, Joe answered, "The nigga told me everything. He told the feds that he could set up a coke deal with this kingpin cat and that he was willing to wear a wire. He told me that the guy he was gonna set up would kill him if he found out, so he was gonna let his little cousin imitate his voice on the tape. He said that he had a kilo that belonged to the guy in one of their stash houses because he used to work for him. He was gonna turn that key in to the feds like he had copped it from him".

Murda zoned out for a second, remembering the three bricks that he had dropped off in Dru Hill for Bang Bang to have cooked up. He started piecing the puzzle together. He figured that Bang Bang was gonna steal the remaining two bricks, sell them, and use the cash to relocate somewhere O.T. After realizing that he had heard everything that he needed to know, Murda walked away from the vent and laid down on his mat. His main objective had become making a call out to the streets and having Bang Bang dealt with ASAP.

❖ ❖

Promise went to work on Monday morning with only five dollars in her pocket. Her menstrual cycle started that morning so she wasn't really the pro-social type at work that day. She had minor cramps, plus a million things on her mind. At a forefront in her mind was the money that she so desperately needed to accept from Murda. By her lunch break at 12:30, she had decided to text Bloodbath and ask him to meet with her when she got off at 5:00. He agreed to meet her on Copeland Street in Annapolis, around 6:15. Then she went to Burger King and spent her last five dollars on lunch. The rest of her cash was set aside for her apartment.

She found it peculiar that Murda hadn't called her again because she knew that he was missing her. She decided that, if he didn't call that Monday, she was gonna call the jail that Tuesday to check on him. That was the least that she could do, provided that he did offer her 20 grand. When the clock struck 5:00, Promise grabbed her time-card and clocked-out in a hurry. She couldn't wait to shoot out to Annapolis, pick up the cash, then retire to her bed for some much-needed rest.

As she walked to her car, she called Xena to check on Zaire and to let her know that she would be running a little late. Realizing that she had an hour to kill, she visited a local furniture store to get a general idea of just how much she was gonna spend. When she calculated the cost for a nice living-room set, a cherry wood bedroom set, and a cherry wood dinette set, she realized that she would have approximately $10,000 remaining. She had planned to use the rest of the cash to self-publish her book as soon as she got finished writing it.

Around 6:00, she called Bloodbath to remind him to meet with her. He was already en route to their meeting spot. When he finally arrived, he followed Promise to the house and they both walked inside. As soon as she walked inside, she caught a quick flashback of her last night in the house. It sent a chill through her body and that's when she told Bloodbath, "It feels creepy in here. Let me just grab a few things from upstairs so we can hurry up and get out of here". She knew that Murda wouldn't mind so she asked Bloodbath to grab the television sets out of Murda's room and Zaire's room. Then put them in the backseat of her Beamer. As he carried them outside, Promise walked upstairs to retrieve the cash from the safe.

When Promise opened the safe, she found two stacks of bills. One stack was all $100 bills and the other stack was all $50 bills. She quickly grabbed both stacks and put them into her black Coach Bucket bag that she was carrying. On her way out of the room, she noticed Murda's jewelry and his cell phone, still sitting on the nightstand near the bed. She placed them in her bag, in hopes that Murda's phone was unlocked so that she could pry and see what other bones she could find in his closet. Then she proceeded down the stairs. Bloodbath had already loaded both televisions into her backseat and was downstairs waiting in the living-room. That's when they walked outside to their vehicles and prepared to leave.

Bloodbath's candy apple-red Cadillac Escalade was parked behind Promise's BMW so he had to back out of the driveway first. Just as he was backing out, two black unmarked Crown Victorias appeared out of nowhere. They both pulled up and parked behind Bloodbath, blocking him in. Then two white men, dressed in civilian clothes, approached both vehicles. They flashed their badges and demanded that they both stepped out of their vehicles, just as two more unmarkeds were arriving on the scene.

Bloodbath didn't resist at all because he knew that he was clean and that he was licensed to be carrying the .45 Ruger that was in his console. Plus, the clip was already ejected out of it. As he stepped out of his truck, with both hands raised in clear view, he warned the officers, "There's a gun in my console and my paperwork for it is in the glove compartment". He allowed the officers to handcuff him as they began conducting their search.

As soon as Promise stepped out of her car, one officer immediately asked her for some identification. When she presented her driver's license to him, he ordered her to turn around and he placed her under arrest. When she asked why she was being apprehended, the officer replied, "For conspiracy and money laundering".

Promise had no idea of what that meant. She had never been arrested before. She was afraid to death, knowing that they were about to find the cash in her purse which could only have made matters worse. Tears were streaming down Promise's face as she was cuffed and placed in the backseat of a transport unit. Bloodbath was sitting on the lawn, just as confused as Promise was. Promise watched nervously as one of the officers rummaged through her purse on the hood of her car. She knew that he had discovered the cash when he called the other officers over and they all laughed as if they had just struck gold. She then noticed one of the officers putting her and Murda's cell phones into a plastic Ziploc bag. She became even more worried then because she knew that, once they reviewed Murda's call records, they would discover even more dirt. And, by her having the phone in her possession, that would automatically put her in collusion.

Bloodbath was un-cuffed after the cops searched his truck but he couldn't leave just yet because his truck was still blocked in. He walked over to the transport unit and told Promise to call his cell phone as soon as they allowed her to make a collect call.

As soon as Bloodbath left, he drove out to the B Hive off of Russelltown Road in Baltimore. He hooked up with Spark to collect some money that he had for Murda. Spark's job was to pick up the cash from Murda's crack spot in Park Heights every week. Murda was too organized to even step one foot on the premises. Spark gave Bloodbath approximately $105,000, which was actually less than what that spot grossed on an average week. With Murda being locked away, some of his workers were slacking on their jobs. Bloodbath knew that Murda would want him to use that money to bail Promise out.

Promise arrived at the Baltimore City Jail around 8:30 that night. She didn't know what to expect as she walked through the corridors leading to the bookings area, escorted by two female officers. She was placed in a small holding cell by herself and she had to wait there until the booking officers were ready to book her in. The cell was extremely cold and she was wearing a short-sleeved shirt. She tucked her arms in her shirt to warm herself up. Then she buried her face in her lap and sobbed for over an hour.

Sporadically, she would walk up to the narrow window on her cell-door where she had a view of the bookings desk. She saw a few detainees being fingerprinted, looking as if they had been waiting in their cells for days. Thoughts of Zaire were weighing heavily on her mind and she whispered a few silent prayers to try and calm her nerves. After almost four hours in that cell, Promise heard a key being turned, opening her cell-door. That's when she raised her head from her lap and waited to see who was about to come inside.

This Hispanic female officer stood in the doorway and asked, "Do you need to make a call?" With dry tears on her face, she sniveled and answered the woman, "Yes ma'am". The officer told her that she could make one collect call so she stood up and put her arms back through her sleeves. When she asked how long she would be there, the woman told her that she would be going before a judge at 9:00 a.m. for a bond consideration. Promise walked over to the payphones that were a few feet away from the bookings desk. The first person that she tried to call was Xena, almost certain that she would be waiting by the phone and probably worried to death.

Xena answered after the first ring and accepted the call without hesitation. Promise was relieved to hear her best friend's voice. Zaire was asleep so Promise didn't bother to wake him up. She explained why she was arrested, to the best of her knowledge, and that she would be seeing a judge in about nine hours. Xena assured her that she would be there and that she would do everything within her powers to get her out of there. Promise was still teary-eyed as she spoke to Xena, but she pulled herself together. Xena made her promise that she would be strong for her, then they ended their conversation and Promise returned to her cell.

It was almost 4:30 a.m. when Promise's cell-door opened again. This time, the same female officer asked her to come over to the bookings desk so that she could be fingerprinted and processed in. The booking process took almost thirty minutes. Then she had to take a mug shot which would appear on her inmate wristband. The officer furnished her with a white blanket and escorted her back to her cell. That's when Promise sat down on the bench, threw the blanket over her shoulders, and tried to go to sleep with her face buried in her lap.

9

TROUBLED ANGEL

At 7:00 a.m., the shift changed and one of the relieving officers took Promise's blanket as soon as he came to work. Then she was offered a cold breakfast tray which she refused off top. Around 8:00, a young black female officer opened the door and told Promise to step out of her cell because she was about to see the judge for a bond hearing. She was placed in ankle-chains and her hands were cuffed to a chain that wrapped around her waist. She and five men were then escorted down a long hallway and into the same small courtroom where Murda's bond hearing was held.

As soon as Promise entered the courtroom, she noticed that Xena was sitting on the back row. She was dressed in her relaxed wear: a pair of sweats, a t-shirt, some white Air Force Ones and a Louis Vuitton headscarf. It was obvious that she was not a morning person. There were two tables in front of the judge's bench. Promise was told to sit down at one table by herself, while the five men were all ordered to sit at the other table. As the judge entered the room, the court officer instructed everyone in the room, "All rise". Everyone stood, including the inmates' family members who were there for moral support. Then the judge said, "You may be seated".

The judge began with one of the men who was arrested for possession with intent to distribute crack-cocaine. When Promise saw the way that he so easily denied his bond, and his blatant disdain for drug offenders, she got shook. As the judge was reading out the charges for the next man, the sound of a door closing resonated in the court room. That's when almost everyone looked back to see who had just entered the courtroom. To Promise's surprise, it was Bloodbath along with Murda's personal lawyer, Mark Nettles. They sat down on the last row, a few seats away from Xena.

Promise kept her head down, too embarrassed to look Xena or Bloodbath in their faces. When the judge began reading her charges out, her heart started thumping. He read from her warrant that she was apprehended on counts of conspiracy and money laundry, and that over $50,000 worth of unaccounted cash was found on her person at the time of her arrest. All eyes shifted in Promise's direction. The judge beamed in on her with a look of sheer disgust, and rendered his decision, "Your bond is set for $75,000 cash or $150,000 surety". Promise dropped her head while struggling to keep her tears at bay, feeling like it would be impossible to come up with that kind of cash.

After the bond hearing, Promise was taken back to her cell. The court officer wouldn't allow her to speak to Xena, Blood-bath or Mark. She was really starting to feel like her entire world was falling apart. She realized that she was about to lose her job because she was scheduled to work at 7:00 that morning.

That was gonna ruin her plans of moving into her own spot because she could no longer afford to pay her monthly rent. She had also fucked up the furniture-money, plus she knew that Murda would be pissed because she had turned over his lawyer-money and his cell phone to the feds. That, on top of the fact that all of their whips were probably confiscated and their house would probably soon be auctioned off.

Promise worried in that cell for hours, hoping that the feds didn't find Murda's Hi-Point .380 under the mattress, leaving her with yet another possible charge. She paced back and forth, waiting to be dressed out and taken to a pod. Around 12:00 p.m., she heard her cell-door being opened so she turned around to see who it was. That's when a white male c.o. asked, "Promise Heyward?" She replied, "Yes sir, that's me". "C'mon, you're being released."

Promise could not believe her ears. "Who could've posted my bail?", she wondered. It took almost thirty minutes for her to be processed out. Then she was escorted out of the jail, carrying nothing but a copy of her warrants and her release papers. She didn't have any property because the feds had kept her Coach bag for evidence. When Promise walked outside, she immediately noticed Bloodbath's Escalade parallel parked on the street, directly behind Mark Nettles' all-white Chrysler 300. Both men were standing next to Bloodbath's truck.

Mark approached Promise with his arm outstretched to shake her hand. Realizing that she probably had a rough night, he simply handed her his business card. Then he told her to give him a call as soon as she got some rest so that he could fully explain her status and instruct her on everything that she needed to do. That's when they hopped in their rides, and Bloodbath took Promise to meet Xena at the Fort Meade military post.

❖ ❖

Earlier that morning, around 6:15, Murda was taken out of the MSU and allowed to return to general population. Only this time, he was taken to an entirely different pod and was red flagged from the man that he was fighting with. He was assigned to another one-man cell without any of his property. He had to wait until the first shift's lieutenant came in at 7:00 to retrieve his property from the Property Control Room. A few minutes before he was let out for 7:30 rec, the lieutenant brought his property to him, along with a clean jumpsuit. He couldn't wait to hop in the shower since it had been two days and the pepper spray was still irritating his skin and his eyes.

Murda didn't know who might've had beef with him in that pod. There were quite a few inmates watching him from their cell-doors when the MSU officer escorted him into the pod. He couldn't make out any faces because of how narrow the glass-windows were on their doors. Their view of him was much clearer than his view of them. He assumed that the guy that he was fighting with was a crip because of the comment that he had made about Murda being a slob. He didn't know if the news about their fight had reached the crips in that pod so he felt the need to get strapped before the c.o. opened his door for rec.

He looked around his cell for any type of sharp object that he could possibly use for a weapon, but to no avail. One thing was for sure, he wasn't about to let anybody have him all scared and cooped up in that cell. He could've stayed in the MSU and checked-in on PC for all that. His only option was to grab two bars of Jergens soap out of his hygiene bag, and he dropped them into a tube sock. Then he tied the sock into a knot so that the soap wouldn't be able to fall out. If something popped off, he was just gonna swing-out with that shit like a pair of nun chucks, on some real Bruce Lee shit.

The c.o. began opening doors on Murda's row and he stood at his door, waiting vigilantly. The sock was concealed in his pocket, clutched tightly in his fist. His jumpsuit and his shower bag were in his left hand. Murda walked out of his cell with a mean mug on his face. Only two other inmates came out for rec so far and he didn't recognize either one of them so he proceeded to the shower. He walked into the cleanest shower that he could find and then shifted the latch to lock the shower-door from the inside. The shower-door was only about 3 1/2 feet-long, blocking his body from his neck to his knees. It was unlikely that someone would run up on him in the shower, but he faced the shower-door for the entire time just incase.

Murda dried-off and got dressed after taking a twenty-minute shower. Then he concealed his weapon in his pocket and stepped out, looking carefully in every direction. Murda was shocked when he spotted his cousin Cool parked in front of the four tvs in the center of the pod. He approached him from behind and scared the shit out of him. That was because he touched him on his right-shoulder and asked, "What's up with that gangsta shit that you were talking nigga?" Cool jerked away and reached for the knife in his waist as he rose to his feet and turned around. That's when he saw Murda about to cough up a lung from laughing so hard.

Cool barked, "C'mon bruh, you can't be playing like that in here. My heart was in my shower-shoes just now".

Then he laughed it off and gave Murda a brotherly hug, followed by a blood handshake. That's when Cool continued, "I got your kite the other day. Whoever set you up is definitely gonna be pushing up daisies as soon as we find out who it is. And good look on the commissary too fam".

Murda replied, "C'mon, real niggas do real things".

"So what are they saying about your case?"

"They want me to cop out to a dime son. This shit is brazy"

"Yea, I know", Cool agreed.

Murda was about to tell Cool what he had found out about Bang Bang, but he paused at midsentence because something on the television screen had caught his attention. "Man, what the fuck?", he thought out loud. Then he walked closer to the television set and realized that his house was on the WBAL-TV Channel 11 news. Cool joined him in front of the tube and tried to figure out what was going on, commanding the men at the card-table to shut the fuck up. A black reporter named Wanda Draper was standing on his front lawn and giving her report. Suddenly, Promise's mug shot popped up on the screen and Murda freaked out.

Murda turned up the volume and caught the end of what Mrs. Draper had to say. She made it seem like Promise was still in custody, obviously unaware that she had conjured up the bond money so fast. He didn't hear what she was charged with but he did hear the cost for her bond. He also heard her say that the house and all of the vehicles were seized until the outcome of her case was decided.

Murda was flabbergasted. He only had about ten minutes left on rec, so he rushed over to the payphone to give Mark Nettles a call. Mark accepted his call without hesitation.

"Mark, you've gotta get down here and get my girl out of jail", Murda demanded.

Mark calmly replied, "Mr. Reed, that's already taken care of. Your girl is out on the streets, safe and sound. Your man Bloodbath paid $15,000 cash on a $150,000 surety bond. It almost got ugly because the judge almost revoked her bond after realizing that her home was being seized and that she no longer had a mailing address for the courts to contact her. That's when I stepped up and put the onus on myself, telling the judge that she would be living with me."

Murda couldn't believe that Mark had finally done something right for a change. That earned him a few points even though he was still on his shit list for not getting him and his workers out yet. That's when Murda said, "I'm still gonna send somebody to your office with that cash, I just gotta make a few calls".

"Yes sir, Mr. Reed", said Mark, now feeling like he had bought himself some more time. Then they ended their conversation and Mark hung up the phone with a big smile plastered across his face.

Promise arrived at the base at roughly 2:00 that afternoon. As soon as she got into Xena's car, she asked her to swing by the commissary so that she could try to retain her job. Even though she looked a hot mess, she walked into the building and directly to her manager's office. He was this older white guy with white hair and craters all in his face. He was very stern, and he ran the commissary with a tight lip. He used to be a drill sergeant. Promise knew that she really didn't stand a chance.

When she began to explain why she couldn't make it in to work that morning, he abruptly interrupted. "Ms. Heyward, there's no need to explain. We all saw the news and read the papers. Sergeant Smith (Antiwan) already stuck his neck out to get you this job and now you've disgraced him, the whole staff here, and the entire U.S. military by doing what you did. Your services will no longer be useful here, and I'm gonna have to terminate you". Promise tried to beg for her job back but he cut her off and threatened, "Please exit my office now before I call security to escort you off the premises".

Promise stared at him with piercing eyes, appalled at how insensitive and merciless he was. Tears began to well-up in her eyes once again and she almost reached her boiling point. That's when she gave up and trampled out of the office. A few of her colleagues that she had gotten cool with were watching her like she was some serial killer who had just pulled off an elaborate con. She was so humiliated that she just dropped her head and left the building without bothering to explain herself.

When Promise returned to Xena's car, she could tell by her demeanor that she had gotten fired. She just drove her home and remained silent for the entire five minutes. When they walked inside, Zaire immediately dropped his G.I. Joe action figure and lunged into Promise's arms. Antiwan placed his hand on Promise's shoulder and asked, "Are you alright?" She replied, "Yes, I'm fine". Then she squeezed Zaire a little bit tighter and kissed him on his cheeks. "I just need a shower and a few hours of rest", Promise continued. That's when she placed Zaire back on his feet and proceeded to the bedroom to prepare to take a hot shower and a nap.

10

GUILTY CONSCIENCE

Promise slept until about 10:00 p.m. Xena had fed Zaire, bathed him, and put him in bed with her sons. Promise decided that it was too late to call Mr. Nettles when she woke up so she turned on her laptop to check her email messages and to work on her book for a while. As soon as she logged in, she noticed that she had two new messages. The first message was sent from a publishing company called Top Flight Publishing. They were responding to the cover letter that she had attached to the six chapters that she had emailed to them. They said that they were willing to print her book but they were a subsidy-press publishing company, meaning that she would have to pay them to manufacture her book.

The second email message was sent from the address, Donnawilkes@verizon.net. It read:

Hello Ms. Heyward, My name is Donna,
chief editor at Angel Baby Publishing. I
have reviewed the six chapters that you sent
to us and I want to let you know that your
book is a sizzling read. Your story was
very touching and I can't wait to read
the finished product. Unfortunately, here
at Angel Baby, we don't publish autobiog-
raphies. We specialize in urban fiction.
However, I do have a very close friend that
I believe will be interested in publishing
your book. May I have your permission to
forward your first six chapters to them?"
-Donna Wilkes.

Promise didn't see any harm in having her manuscript forwarded, so she replied, "Sure, you can forward my book and
thanks for your help." She double-clicked on the Microsoft
Word icon and began typing in her book. She could barely even
concentrate, thinking about her court situation and her finan-
cial situation. She only had $1,200 to her name, the money
that she had saved from working at the commissary. She had
no car, no job and no permanent place to call home. She had
been crashing with Xena and Antiwan for over a month and
she was starting to feel like she was wearing-out her welcome.

By the time that she decided to turn off her laptop, almost
two hours later, she hadn't even typed three complete para-
graphs. That's when she walked into the living-room to get
Zaire. He and the other two boys were sleeping in the pull-out
couch-bed. Promise laid in her bed and stared at her son as he
slept next to her. He was sleeping peacefully, like he didn't have
a care in the world.

The last thing on Promise's mind was giving up or giving
in. Remnants of her mother's voice echoed in her head, "You're

too blessed to be stressed and too anointed to be disappointed". That's when Promise recited her usual serenity prayer and turned off the lamp. Then she kissed Zaire on his forehead and whispered to him, "Don't worry, mommy's gonna make a way Za Za. I promise."

Promise fell asleep with her arm wrapped around Zaire. She didn't wake up until around 9:30 the next morning. Since Zaire was still sleeping, she grabbed Mr. Nettles' business card from the nightstand and gave him a call at his office. Mark explained the dynamics of her case and what she needed to do. He said that if she wanted to win her case in trial, she had the burden of proving that the house and all of Murda's cars were purchased with legal money that belonged to her. The feds had done a thorough investigation and a F.D.I.C. check. There was no record of Promise being employed anywhere during the times when the house and the cars were bought, so she had one hell of a fight on her hands.

Xena overheard Promise talking to Mr. Nettles as she was walking past her bedroom. As soon as Promise hung up the phone, Xena knocked softly on the door. "Come in", Promise stated in a melancholy voice. As Xena entered the room, she said, "Hey, I was just wondering if you and Zaire wanted to join me for breakfast at Denny's". Promise felt too embarrassed to accept the offer but Xena insisted. That's when they all got dressed and drove out to Denny's on Ritchie Highway in Glen Burnie, right next to the DMV.

Xena and Promise both ordered a Belgian Waffle, a Veggie-cheese omelette and some Tropicana orange juice to drink. Promise ordered a kid's meal for Zaire. As they talked over breakfast, Promise started to explain that she was feeling sorry for Murda and considering holding him down. She expressed that she was feeling like she had made his predicament even worse by giving the feds his phone and his money. Xena threw up her index finger, as if to say, "Wait one minute until i finish chewing my food". Then she washed it down with a gulp of orange juice and exclaimed, "Promise, fuck Murda okay?!"

Promise looked at Zaire, then back at Xena. That's when Xena apologized for her profanity, "My fault, but really....think about it. It was his idea for you to go back to that house in the first place. If anyone has the right to be mad, it's you. That nigga was using you the whole time, just to put shit in your name. Just pay attention to the signs Promise, it's written all over the wall. He blacked your eye, he cheated on you, he's facing life, and now he's got you tangled up in this shit. It's not meant to be, and God is trying to show you that."

"Maybe you're right", said Promise.

Then she said, "I just don't know what I'm gonna do. I don't have a job, I don't have a man, I don't have nothing".

Her voice dropped an octave as she placed her eyes on Zaire and continued, "but my son."

A young white waitress approached them and placed their bill on the table. That's when Promise began fumbling through her Chanel bag. Xena figured that she was trying to pay for her and Zaire's food, so she said, "I told you that I was gonna foot the bill".

Promise then said, "I know but...." That's when she withdrew a white envelope from her bag and slid it across the table to Xena.

When Xena cracked it open, she found five crispy $100 bills. Then she asked, "What's this for?"

Promise said that the money was for her letting them stay with her and Antiwan.

"Don't ever insult me like that again", said Xena, sliding the envelope right back to her.

"I could never take anything from you, knowing everything that you are going through. So put that money right back in your bag and you can stay with us for as long as you need to."

Promise's heart melted at that very moment, realizing how good of a friend Xena was. She got all emotional and teary-eyed. "I love you girl", Promise said flatly.

Then Xena replied, "I love you too girl".

They both rose to their feet and hugged each other. After a few seconds, Xena pulled away and said, "Alright, that's enough of this mushy shit. These people in here are gonna think we're lesbians". They both chuckled and grabbed their things to prepare to leave. Xena walked over to the cashier to pay for the food and Promise approached one of the managers to ask if they were hiring. He said that they would be hiring soon so she asked for an application. Then they hopped back in Xena's Lexus and headed back to Fort Meade.

❖ ❖

That same Wednesday afternoon, Mark Nettles went to visit Murda. He gave him a copy of the lab reports stating that the cocaine tested positive and that it weighed exactly 1,008 grams. He also had a tape recorder and a copy of the audio tape. When he played the tape for Murda, both voices were clearly audible and the buyer definitely sounded like Bang Bang. Murda couldn't make out the other voice. Strangely, Bang Bang kept saying the names J.R. and Joe, obviously to convince the feds that J.R. stood for Joseph Reed. For a second, he worried that Bang Bang might've given the investigators a tip about the kid J.R., who they had tortured to death on Reisterstown Road. Nettles also said that Promise could receive up to 240 months in the feds if she was found guilty of her charges.

After Murda's lawyer visit, he called Spark and told him to visit him on Thursday afternoon. When he came, Murda told him to deliver $30,000 to Mark so that he could try to pay-off the solicitor. Then he told him to find Bang Bang and have him dealt with. He knew that Bang Bang was a snake and, if allowed to live, he would only sting someone else. Meanwhile, Bang Bang had sold both keys for a quick 35 grand and he relocated to Newport News, Virginia. He knew that the word would've eventually got out so he slid. The feds ordered him to call them once a week and to report to them once a month until the date of Murda's arraignment.

Murda knew what time it was and he knew that Spark and his other soldiers would never catch up to Bang Bang. He also knew that Bang Bang would be expecting him to plead to the ten-year plea bargain instead of risking a life sentence in a trial, just to find out who the confidential informant was. Murda brainstormed for hours that night. That's when he decided that if his lawyer couldn't pay-off the solicitor, he was gonna take it to trial just so that Bang Bang would have to appear in court. Then he was planning to have Bang Bang wacked either before the hearing, or right after the trial was adjourned. It was that serious to him. He would just have to try to get his sentence overturned through appeals.

Spark delivered the cash to Mark bright and early Friday morning. Plus he put out APB's for Bang Bang in all Blood territories throughout the city. His head was worth 100 stacks. Murda and all of his workers were waiting on successive bond hearings in the next ninety days. He knew that he wasn't going anywhere until then, so he told Spark to put a few stacks on his books so that he could stock up on food and hygiene.

Since Murda didn't have a number to contact Promise at, his only choice was to wait until she decided to visit him. He still had three crack spots that were thriving and he was forced to trust Spark to keep everything in order. After a week in that pod, Murda and Cool got with one of the lieutenants and requested to be cellmates since they were cousins. Once they moved in a cell together, time seemed to speed up for them. They got along, ate good, and watched each other's backs at all times. They worked-out everyday and, after a few weeks, they both got on some real diesel shit.

Mark visited Murda frequently to inform him of all progress in his case. He had no info on who the confidential informant was but that was no longer a mystery to Murda. He just didn't reveal his findings to Mark so, when Bang Bang turned up dead, he wouldn't have any idea that he had ordered the hit. Murda and Cool became looked-at as the dons in that pod. They both maxed-out on the canteen's weekly spending limit every week. It seemed like Murda's rep was growing even bigger behind the g-walls.

After the officers recognized just how much cash he was playing with, most of them wanted to jump onboard and make a little bit of extra change. In a matter of thirty days, Murda had five different mules. They brought him street-food on the regular, an I-Pod, a cell phone, Newports and PCP, lighters, weed and coke to flood the jail with. Since they didn't have cash in the jail, Murda had to go digital. He ordered a few pre-paid Rush Cards and made his custees pay him with Green Dot reload money packs. All they had to do was get their people to pick them up from a local Walgreens, give them the pin code from the back of the card, and they could pay Murda with that. Once Murda loaded their money onto his Rush Cards, then he would give them their product.

Murda paid Spark and all of his mules well because the coke-flip in jail was beautiful. In there, coke went for $100 a gram, easily. That was almost three stacks per ounce and he was only paying $18,000 a brick because he was buying volume. So he was turning $18,000 into $108,000. That means that he was flipping his cash 60%. He never knew that the coke flip behind the walls was so sweet. While other inmates were eating chow from the mess-hall, Murda and Cool were in their cell eating like kings and watching the latest movies on their Android smart phones. Promise never went to visit Murda but he stopped giving a fuck. He was too concerned with getting money.

There were a few other bloods in the pod that Murda would look out for, even though they weren't in his set. They were Sex, Money and Murder niggas, a set based out of NYC. Murda even got fly with a female officer who worked third shift. She liked getting her nose dirty so Murda would hit her off. In return, she would creep to Murda's cell late at night and give him and Cool some top, or let them fuck her. She was a tall and sexy redbone named Erica, from East Baltimore.

Other inmates were starting to hate but that shit didn't faze Murda. Cool's birthday came around so they both went up on the top tier and made it rain oatmeal pies on them broke-ass niggas. They had jailhouse shanks while Murda and Cool had real box cutters and Rambo knives from the street. Plus, there were so many bloods in that pod that nobody would think about jumping stupid.

11

THE BIG DAY

Two months had passed since Promise's arrest and she still wasn't dating anyone yet. She had landed a new job as a crew manager at Dick's sporting goods in the Glen Burnie Mall. She moved into her own crib in Bowie a month earlier and she was slowly buying furniture piece by piece. Xena let her use her Honda Civic, temporarily, until she could afford to buy her own car. Promise had finally finished writing her book and she was constantly looking for new publishers to submit her manuscript to. She had mentioned her court situation and all of her drama with Murda in her last three chapters.

Promise had also begun reporting to court every Tuesday morning for roll call because her name was added to the court docket. Mark Nettles told her that her reporting was only routine court procedure and that her actual arraignment would probably be over six months later.

One Thursday evening after a long day at work, Promise drove to the Fort Meade military post to pick up Zaire from Xena. Then she drove home to get some rest. When she walked into her crib, she checked her email messages as she usually did, hoping that some publisher was ready to make her a hefty offer to release her book. The only message that she found was another message from Donna Wilkes. This time, she said that her publisher-friend also wanted to read her finished product and that they were interested in printing her book, based on what they had read so far.

Promise had a few extra dollars so she went online to the Library of Congress' website and paid, by credit card, to have Troubled Angel copyrighted. Then she emailed the entire manuscript to Donna, crossing her fingers. "I hope they like it", she thought out loud. Then she put Zaire to bed and went into her own room to try to get some sleep. Thoughts of Murda began to linger in the deep recesses of her mind as she wondered how he was holding up in jail. She knew that he would've reached out to her by then, had he known her new cell number. She was actually missing him but her conscience kept telling her to stay away from him.

She was living like a total square with no type of social life at all. All she did was eat, sleep and work. Deep down, she was still afraid because she didn't know how her court situation was gonna turn out. She still hadn't figured out an alibi to use. Mark was looking for loopholes in her case on his end, trying to find any type of procedural errors that the cops might've made at the time of her arrest. Unfortunately, they had written up the incident report perfectly. Promise just tried to stay prayed-up about the whole situation.

One week later, on that Friday evening, Promise thought that God had begun answering her prayers. She returned home from work and realized that she had received a new message from Donna Wilkes. Donna had sent her contact number and said that her publisher-friend wanted to meet with them both to discuss signing a contract. Promise called her immediately and they arranged a rendezvous over lunch that Saturday, at Fleming's Prime Steakhouse & Wine Bar on Aliceanna Street in Baltimore. Promise jotted down the restaurant's address and assured Donna that she would be there at 12:30 p.m., sharp. After hearing Donna's voice , Promise realized that she was a white woman.

Early the next morning, Promise asked Xena to watch Zaire while she attended her meeting. She wanted to make a good first impression so she took Xena's Honda Civic to be detailed, then she drove back home to get dressed. She wanted to look exquisite so she put on this sexy but classy all-black Alexander McQueen dress and a pair of all-black Jimmy Choo heels. The micro-braids in her hair were still practically fresh. Plus, she threw on a pair of black Marc Jacobs shades and a black and gold Cartier wrist-watch.

She arrived at Fleming's Prime Steakhouse & Wine Bar at 12:30 sharp. Donna arrived shortly afterwards and they both seemed excited to be meeting in person. "I just spoke with him and he's running a little late. He said for us to just order whatever we wanted and that he'll be here shortly", Donna said to Promise. "I'm starved", she continued, as they began walking towards the restaurant's entrance. Donna was dressed to impress, rocking a Donna Karan cut-out dress and a pair of matching Charlotte Olympia heels. The restaurant was a very casual setting, with soft music playing and a plethora of uppity white folks all around.

The greeter gave both of them two menus each. One menu was for the food, and the other menu had 100 different wines for them to choose from. Then a young white waitress escorted them to a table right next to the store-front window that they had parked near. Donna seemed goofy as hell but Promise laughed at all of her corny punch lines, trying to be cordial.

Promise and Donna both looked over their menus for a few minutes until that same waitress returned with a pen and pad in hand.

"Are you ladies ready to order?" she asked, giving a courteous smile.

"Yes, I'd like a Prime Bone-In Rib Eye Steak and some Twin Australian Lobster Tails", said Donna, practically drooling at the mouth.

"And what would you like to drink?", the waitress asked.

Donna shrugged and answered, "I don't know, how about a glass of Bordeaux's Concord Grape Wine?"

Promise looked at the menu and calculated the cost for Donna's order in her head. Her food alone cost over $70. She didn't want to seem greedy so she hesitated to order. That's when Donna said, "Girl don't be bashful. Money's no object with this guy".

Then Promise placed her order, "Well give me the same order as hers but I'll take a glass of Merlot's Red Wine to drink".

As the waitress walked away to prepare their orders, Donna gazed out of the window and thought out loud, "Well....speaking of the devil". Promise gave a cursory glance in the same direction and noticed a very familiar-looking silver and red Lamborghini Sesto Elemento parallel-parking directly behind Donna's black Lexus GS430. Promise's heart almost leaped out of her chest when the driver stepped out and she realized that it was Andre Vasquez, the man that she had a one-night stand with a few months prior.

This time, Andre was dressed like a typical DC cat. He was wearing a Visionz t-shirt, a DC fitted cap, a pair of stone-washed Rock and Republic jeans and a pair of all-black Nike ACG boots. Just as he was making his way inside, Promise grabbed her clutch bag and told Donna, "Excuse me for one second". Then she scurried to the ladies room and checked herself out in the mirror. She was as nervous as hell, hoping that he wouldn't remember her face. She double-checked her hair and her lip gloss, released a deep sigh and said to herself, "Okay Promise, you can do this". Then she threw her Marc Jacobs shades back on and walked back to their table.

Andre was sitting beside Donna when Promise returned. "There she is", said Donna, as Promise walked up from behind them. Andre turned around, reached out his hand and introduced himself. He didn't recognize Promise behind her sunglasses. Promise placed her hand inside his and said, "Hello, I'm Promise Heyward". Promise then removed her shades and Andre couldn't believe his eyes. "Wow...so we finally meet again", he said, smiling from ear to ear. Promise returned the smile and replied, "Yes, how are you?" "You two know each other?", Donna asked. Then Andre said, "Yes, I met her a while back at a book fair."

When Promise realized that Andre wasn't about to put her on blast, she played along with him and continued on with their meeting. Their platters arrived so they didn't get straight down to business. Andre wasn't hungry so he just ordered himself a glass of Dom Perignon while the ladies enjoyed their lunches.

Andre admired Promise's beautiful face and her figure-eight frame as he took a few sips from his glass. He zoned-out for a second, thinking back on that night at his house when he and Promise had sex. Promise's pheromones seemed to be screaming out at him because he was rocking-up and fantasizing about lying her down for a second time. Promise was deliberately avoiding eye contact because she too was thinking about that explosive night that they had spent together.

Promise diverted, "So, you liked my manuscript?"

Snapping out of his daze, he replied, "Sure, I loved it. That's why we're here".

Donna picked up on the vibe because there was an awkward silence at their table. She decided to give them some privacy so she excused herself from the table and walked to the ladies' room.

That's when Andre placed his glass on a coaster and asked, "So why didn't you ever call me, ma? Did you lose my card?"

She replied, "Because I didn't know how you were gonna look at me after we did what we did. To be honest, I was too embarrassed".

"You have no reason to be embarrassed. I was just as guilty as you were. I thought that you might've looked at me like some dog-ass nigga or something", Andre stated.

Then Promise laughed, "Yeah but you're a dude and that's expected. But me, I played myself". Andre believed that he had represented in the bedroom that night but, after that last comment, he was starting to wonder if he'd really satisfied her. That's when Promise affirmed, "I'm not saying that the sex was whack or anything. I was just going through some things at the time and I really shouldn't have done that. I just got caught up in the moment".

Andre realized that Promise was getting uncomfortable because they were discussing a delicate topic, so he switched subjects. "So, your book...it was a definite page-turner. The way that you detailed everything and painted such a vivid picture, I would've thought that you were writing about your own life".

"I was", she confided. Andre grew silent, remembering a few of the tragic scenes in her book. The ones that had touched him the most were the gruesome death of her pops, Dottie, and the loss of her mother, Treasure.

"Wow...I would've never guessed that your story was that deep. I thought that you were just some rich girl when I first saw you. You were rocking Chanel diamond earrings with a gold Cartier watch."

Promise cut Andre off right then, realizing that their conversation was going too deep into her personal life. She knew that pretty soon she would have to bring up Murda and that was a chapter that she wasn't quite ready to delve into. Donna returned to the table after almost five minutes in the ladies' room. As she was sitting back down, Promise asked Andre, "So, what are the terms of the contract?"

Andre normally paid his new authors a $10,000 signing bonus for their freshman release, plus 70% royalties for every book that was sold. He was really feeling Promise.He was touched by her story and was feeling pressured to wanna help her in any way possible. That's when he answered, "I'm willing to pay you $20,000 upfront to sign with True Life Publishing, plus I'll give you 75% royalties on every book that we sell. I'll cover all of the marketing and the promotion as well".

Promise was ecstatic to hear the good news but she held her composure. All she could see were dollar signs. That's when she suddenly remembered an old saying that her college professor, Mr. Propst, used to say, "Real success is finding your lifework in the work that you love". For the first time, she was starting to feel like she had found her purpose in life, to be a writer just like her mother.

"So, where do I sign?", Promise asked without faltering. Andre grabbed a contract from his briefcase that was on the floor between his legs. Then he slid one over to Promise so that she could survey it. She read it very carefully, reading all fine print, until she was certain that there were no hidden terms. There was an empty space provided for the amount of the signing bonus. When Promise agreed to join the True Life family, Andre wrote $20,000 in that space and she signed her John Hancock on the dotted line.

"Is this your correct mailing address?", asked Andre, proof-reading her entries.

She answered "Yes, why?"

"Okay, you should be receiving a copy of this contract along with your check in the mail in two to three business days." Andre placed the contract back in his briefcase and the waitress returned with his bill, lying it face-down on the table. Promise just knew that he was gonna freak out when he flipped it over and saw how much it was. He looked at the bill and nonchalantly grabbed his wallet from his back pocket. It was a thick black Tom Ford wallet, packed with cards and a noticeable stack of cash.

When Andre opened his wallet, he quickly withdrew his American Express Black Card. Then he placed it on top of the bill, making sure that Donna and Promise had both seen it. "So did you ladies want anything else because I have to be going?", he asked like a perfect gentleman. They both replied, "No that was plenty." Andre stood up to shake both women's hands. Then he walked over to the cashier to pay the tab. As he exited the restaurant, he gave Promise one last glance. She waved goodbye so he winked back. Promise became so excited that she had lost her appetite. As she watched Andre hop back into his Lambo, she realized that her business there was done. Then she thanked Donna for plugging her in and they both prepared to leave and get back to their own respective lives.

12

RECONSTRUCTION

Promise received her package in the mail that Wednesday afternoon. She had realized that twenty grand wasn't gonna take her very far so she bought a few pieces of furniture and stashed almost $15,000 away for a rainy day. Plus, she continued working at Dick's part-time. That following weekend, Promise received an email message from True Life's in-house graphics designer, named Phil. He was asking Promise what type of concept she had in mind for the cover of her book.

Andre hadn't wasted any time getting started on her book. His editors had already begun doing her layout and her photo-shoot was scheduled for two weeks later. Andre was confident that Troubled Angel would be a good addition to his catalog. The story was heartfelt and he loved Promise's writing style. After reading her story, and finding out that she was the actual author, his attraction to her grew even stronger than it was before. Ever since that night when they first met, he had been waiting patiently for her to call so that he could try to get to know her on a more personal level.

Andre had been single for almost one year, ever since he divorced his ex-wife for messing around with some guy from her past. Since then, he'd been doing the bachelor thing and waiting for Ms. Right to come along. He would frequent casual clubs, searching for a decent woman because he was at that stage where he wanted to settle down and be faithful to one woman. He had plenty of women in his day and women were always throwing themselves at him because of his status and his money. That night when he had slept with Promise was uncanny for the both of them because Andre hadn't had a one-night stand since his divorce.

Promise arrived at her photo-shoot one Saturday afternoon around 2:00. She didn't know what to expect. She was wearing her relaxed wear because she was told that she would be given a complete makeover for her photo-shoot. She just hoped that Andre's personal stylists had good taste.

This particular Saturday was Promise's first time ever visiting True Life Publishing. It was in a small plaza out in Laurel, Maryland. From the outside the company didn't look like much but, once she walked inside, she was definitely convinced that this company was the real deal. There was a white female receptionist sitting at a desk in the lobby area when Promise invited herself inside. She was wearing a white Rugby-style shirt with the True Life logo embroidered on the upper-left side.

"May I help you miss?", asked the receptionist.

"Yes, I have a 2:00 appointment with Mr. Vasquez", Promise replied.

"One moment please", said the receptionist, picking up the phone to dial Andre's extension. Promise began looking around at the many book covers that had been framed and hung on all four walls of the lobby. She was also impressed by the huge company logo that was made into the carpet. "That had to cost a fortune", she thought.

The next thing that Promise noticed was the collection of photos that were in a huge glass frame on the wall near the entrance door. She couldn't believe her eyes when she saw pictures of Andre with some of the top-named black moguls. He had pictures with Denzel Washington, Will Smith and Erykah Badu, just to name a few. She could tell that the photos weren't computer-generated because each star was holding a copy of a book, obviously written by one of the authors signed to his publishing company. Plus, they were all wearing promotional True Life Publishing t-shirts. There were a few faces that she didn't recognize in the pictures, probably other successful authors who weren't as publicized.

Promise became a little nervous when she heard the receptionist telling Andre that he had a guest waiting for him in the lobby. "What did you say your name was again ma'am?", the woman asked. "Promise Heyward", she replied, placing her eyes back on the photos. Then the woman hung up the phone and told Promise that Andre was on his way to the lobby to meet her. Thats when Promise took a seat and waited.

Andre came through the double-doors almost two minutes later, looking like a real CEO. He was clad in a charcoal-gray Salvatore Ferragamo suit and a pair of Louis Vuitton loafers. He had a clean shave and the waves in his hair were so deep that they would make you seasick. When Promise rose to her feet to shake his hand, he kissed her backhand just the way that he did it at the K Street Lounge. "You look marvelous, as always", he said, admiring her flawless face. "Are you serious? I look a hot mess", she replied, blushing. Then he escorted her through the double-doors and gave her a quick tour of the company.

He introduced her to the printing team, the graphics specialist and all four of his editors. Everyone was friendly to her, making her feel right at home.

After her tour, Andre took her to a room where there were two white female make-up artists and a black hair stylist waiting to make her over. He had hired them all personally. Andre instructed all three of them, "Give her whatever she likes." They all agreed and assured him that she was in good hands. That's when he returned to his office to handle some other business. The hair stylist took one look at Promise and suggested a style that she thought would fit her perfectly. She trusted her acumen and let her go to work on her. There were no mirrors in sight and Promise hoped that she would like the style after the woman finished. While she was getting her make-up done, this almost gay-looking guy walked into the room and asked Promise for her dress and shoe sizes. Then he left out of the room and Promise closed her eyes as the make-up artists finished up.

Promise had been sitting in that chair for almost two hours before one of the make-up artists finally said, "Done!" That's when Promise opened her eyes to one of the women holding a mirror up in front of her. Promise couldn't believe her eyes. She had never felt so beautiful before. The hair-stylist had given her a sexy sew-in with Remy hair. Her make-up was really light because she didn't have any blotches in her skin to begin with. They just highlighted her eyes with a little eye-liner and some eye-shadow. They had Promise looking like a Cover Girl model and she was loving it.

The effeminate white guy then walked back into the room, pulling a mobile rack filled with dresses and ten different boxes of female shoes. Promise rushed over to him and began sifting through the dresses. They were all vintage, everything from Oscar de la Renta to Saint Laurent. All of the dresses were white, which happened to be her favorite color. She finally decided on this beautiful bandage dress made by Isabel Marant. Then she picked out a pair of white open-toed heels made by Chelsea Paris, and proceeded to the dressing-room to finish preparing for her photo-shoot.

When Promise walked out of the dressing-room, the three women applauded and told her how stunning she looked. Then the white guy escorted her into a nearby room where there was a photographer waiting for her. The room had been made up like a professional photography studio with expensive lighting equipment, a green screen and a phalanx of hi-definition digital cameras. The photographer was this black guy named Marcus. He shook Promise's hand and began explaining the whole photo-shoot procedure to her.

"Okay, I'm gonna need for you to stand in front of this green screen and we're gonna take ten different poses. Then we'll decide on whichever one you like the most."

Promise then asked, "Does my background have to be green?"

The photographer laughed, realizing that Promise obviously had no idea of what the green screen was for. Then he explained, "That screen is so that the graphics designer can create whatever type of backdrop you want".

Then Promise laughed it off and said, "Okay, let's get on with it."

Just as the photographer was setting the lighting, Andre entered the room to see the work that his stylists had done on Promise. Promise waltzed over to him with a bright smile plastered across her face. "Man, thank you so much for all of this. You're the best", she said, wrapping her arms around him. Andre returned her hug, reminding her that she looked breath-taking. Then Promise walked over to the green screen to begin her photo-shoot. The photographer suggested that, since her book was entitled Troubled Angel, she should pose with a troubled expression on her face. As Promise posed for the camera, Andre just leered at her, feeling more and more like he wanted her to be in his life. Between photo-shots, Promise glanced back at him and she could tell that he loved what he saw. Little did he realize though, Promise was starting to feel for him in the same way.

After Promise took ten different poses, she and Andre walked over to the photographer's laptop so that Promise could select the photo that she liked the most. As they flipped through each one, Andre couldn't restrain himself from staring in adoration. Promise finally decided on a photo and then she explained how she wanted her backdrop to look. She said that she wanted clouds placed behind her since she was dressed in all white, and the book-title was Troubled Angel. Andre said that he thought that was a great idea and Promise was elated.

When the session was over, Andre insisted that Promise wore her outfit home since she looked so beautiful in it. Then Andre walked her to her car. The entire way there, she kept telling him how grateful she was and how excited she was to finally be getting her book printed. When they reached her driver's side door, Andre said, "Hey Promise...I was wondering".

Then Promise looked into his eyes and he continued, "Would you like to go out sometimes?"

Promise thought back to that night they had spent together, hesitating to respond.

That's when he assured her, "This time it will be strictly friendly. That's my word".

Promise could sense the sincerity in his eyes and she did feel comfortable in his company, so she agreed, "Sure, strictly friendly. I think I could use a good friend right now".

"Cool, so how's tomorrow night? Say around 8:00?", Andre asked.

"Eight o'clock sounds fine", she answered. Then she got into her car and drove to meet Xena so that she could pick up Zaire.

The K Street Lounge in DC is where Andre usually spent his Saturday nights at. But, on this particular night, he decided to stay at home and do some reading. Around 6:00 that evening, he opened his email messages and began reading the Troubled Angel manuscript for the second time. He wanted to make their first official date a special one so he read her bio to learn some things that might've had sentimental value to her.

In the early chapters of Promise's book, she wrote about how her parents used to always take her to the Baltimore Inner Harbor as a child. They would do this annually just before school started each year. They would spend the entire day shopping at the Harborplace and the Gallery right on the waterfront. They would also take a cruise of the harbor on what she referred to as the Big Red Boat. At the end of the night, she and her parents would have dinner at Treasure's favorite restaurant called the Capital Grille, right in the heart of the Inner Harbor. In that very same restaurant is where Dottie had proposed to Treasure.

Andre Googled the restaurant's name to find out if it still existed. To his benefit, they were still in business. He then called and made a 9:30 p.m. reservation for the best table in the house, a private alcove table with a beautiful view of the harbor. He inquired to the restaurant's shift manager about the Big Red Boat and he gave him the necessary information that he needed in order to book a cruise. He made arrangements for a ninety minute cruise of the Inner Harbor, figuring that that would be a nice romantic getaway that would allow him and Promise enough time to really talk and get to know each other.

Promise spent that entire evening at home, enjoying the company of her son. Even though she was worried about her court situation, her spirits were really high that evening. She thought about the fact that her book was being published, and she also had a good feeling about her new friend, Andre. She had no clue about where Andre was planning to take her out to but she was excited to be finally dating again. When she told Xena about it, she was more than happy to babysit Zaire while Promise and Andre went out. Xena agreed to pick up Zaire early on Sunday afternoon, on her way home from her church in Laurel.

13

TONIGHT'S THE NIGHT

Xena swung by to pick up Zaire around 2:00 Sunday afternoon. That's when Promise drove out to the Wheaton Mall to buy an outfit to wear on her date. She picked out a white BCBG tube top dress called the Max Azria. Then she bought a pair of BCBG wedge sandals to match the dress. When she finished shopping, she returned home to clean her house and to prepare for her date with Andre.

Time seemed to be moving fast that day and, before she knew it, the sun was setting. Andre had sent her a text message around 6:30, letting her know that he would be at her door at 8:00 sharp. She spent almost 2 hours getting beautified. It was 7:57 pm when Promise's doorbell rung. That's when she took one last glimpse into the mirror and scurried over to the door. When she opened the door, Andre was all smiles, holding a fresh bouquet of white roses. Promise said, "Awe thank you" giving him a friendly hug. That's when she noticed that he was wearing some Prada Luna Rossa cologne.

Promise received the flowers and invited Andre inside while she placed them in a vase with some water. Andre was dressed casually in a white short sleeve Maison-Martin Margiela shirt, a pair of gray stone-washed Kenneth Cole jeans and a pair of Bally suede sneakers with crocodile trim on his feet. He was also wearing a pair of Cazals with gold frames and a gold watch made by Franck Muller. He took a seat in Promise's living room on her new green leather couch while she put the roses in a vase in her bedroom. Then they walked outside to his car.

Promise was expecting to see his Lamborghini parked outside but this time he was driving a cream-colored Jaguar XJ. "I love this car", said Promise as they both walked to the passenger's side door. "This old thing?" he asked in a modest yet sarcastic way. Promise gave a light chuckle as Andre opened the door for her to step inside. Then he walked around the front of the car and hopped into the driver's seat.

This car was laced up, with butter soft leather seats and beautiful wood grain everywhere. Promise felt like she was floating on air because the car rode so smoothly. There wasn't a grain of dirt in sight, plus the air freshener hanging from the rearview mirror had the car smelling like strawberries. When he turned up the music, Promise was shocked to hear the sounds of one of her favorite artists, Musiq Soulchild. That was another idea that he had gotten from her book.

"So, exactly where are we going?", Promise asked. That's when Andre told her that he had made reservations at this particular restaurant, not disclosing the name of it. As they arrived on Pratt Street in front of the Capital Grille, Promise hardly recognized it because they had remodeled a lot since she had last eaten there as a child. Andre paid the valet $75 to park his car for 3 1/2 hours and, then they walked into the restaurant.

When they walked inside, it dawned on Promise where she was at. The inside of the restaurant still looked pretty much the same, very elegant. They were escorted to their reserved table and given two huge menus to order from. Andre ordered himself some lobster and crab cakes, and Wagyu Beef Carpaccio. Promise ordered a shrimp cocktail and pan-fried calamari with hot cherry peppers. They both ordered Bordeaux's red wine to drink.

As they were waiting on their platters to arrive, Promise told Andre that she used to visit that restaurant every year with her parents. That's when he confessed that he had already known that from reading her manuscript.

"I forgot that I even wrote that in there", Promise said, chuckling.

That's when Andre said, "I love your smile".

Promise said "Thank you", then they both focused their attention on the live jazz band that was playing in the restaurant.

When their meals arrived, Promise initiated the conversation. "So, tell me something...you have all these nice cars, plus your own business. What are you doing single?"

Andre took a bite of his Carpaccio and replied, "I was married until about a year ago. I divorced my wife because she was unfaithful".

"Oh, I'm sorry to hear that", said Promise. She could tell by his countenance and direct eye contact that he was telling the truth.

Promise switched subjects and began talking about the times when she and her parents used to visit the harbor back in the days. Andre listened mostly, as Promise shared some of her happiest memories about her childhood. She and Murda had never had a similar conversation because it was all about Murda whenever they spent time together. Promise relished the idea of finally being able to open up to someone besides Xena about any and every thing. When Promise mentioned the death of her parents, Andre said that he too had lost both parents at a young age. They both had died in a vehicular homicide while he was doing a juvenile bid at a group home in Southeast, Washington D.C.

Andre explained that that was his reason for being in the streets at such a young age. He was introduced to selling drugs at the age of twelve and had been in and out of jail from then up until the age of 22. That's when he got released from prison for the last time. Before going to prison, he had stashed over $100,000 of drug money. When he got released, he invested that money into his publishing company and hadn't turned back since. Promise was definitely enthralled by his success story and, so far, their chemistry was good.

When Andre looked down at his Franck Muller and realized that it was almost 10:30, he beckoned the waitress so that she could bring him his bill. He and Promise finished their drinks, and then Andre paid the tab with his American Express Gold card. That's when they both exited the restaurant through the waterfront exit. There was a myriad of other couples walking around the harbor and many memories came to Promise's mind, about walking that very same course with her parents years ago.

"So, where are we going now?", Promise asked. "It's a surprise", Andre replied. Noticing that most of the other couples were holding hands, Andre grabbed Promise's hand as they were walking. She didn't resist at all. She gently placed her hand in his and they looked into each other's eyes. She was tempted to stop in her tracks and give him a kiss smack on the lips but she remembered their pact, strictly friendly.

Within the next ten minutes, they were approaching the pier to board the big red boat which was scheduled to leave at 11:00. As soon as she recognized it, Promise lit up like a light bulb. Her first reaction was to cover her mouth in amazement. "Oh my god, how did you know?" she began, just before wrapping her arms around Andre's neck. He just laughed because that was the reaction that he had expected.

When they boarded the boat, they both walked to one of the enclosed decks where there was a full-service bar, a dining area and a club-like atmosphere. Since they had just eaten, Andre asked Promise if she wanted another drink. She replied, "Sure", so they both took seats at the bar. Andre ordered Promise an apple martini cocktail and he ordered himself a glass of Hennessy and coke. Once they felt that the boat was in motion, they grabbed their drinks and walked out to the open air panoramic deck which gave a wonderful view of the historic harbor.

Promise was feeling a little tipsy by then. That's when they decided to find a section of the deck where they could talk and be alone. Promise took light sips from her glass as she stared at the beautiful view of the stars and Baltimore's World Trade Center. For the most part of the cruise, they held an idle conversation, just joking and having fun talking about their children. Then Andre decided to talk about something more serious.

"So Promise, I have something that I want to ask you".

"Go ahead", she replied, clueless about what it could've been.

Then Andre continued, "When I read your book, in the last few chapters you mentioned being in trouble with the law. Was that true?"

Promise didn't see that one coming. She wondered what was his concern, hoping that her court situation wasn't about to ruin their business relationship. It took her a few moments to muster the courage to just give an honest answer.

"I just got out of a bad relationship with my son's father a few months ago. I was blind back then, thinking that I was in love, while the whole time he was just using me to buy a rack of shit in my name. He got caught selling drugs and they found out that his house and all of his cars were in my name. So, they charged me with conspiracy and money laundering."

Andre remained silent and looked steadily into her eyes as she spilled her heart out.

"I know that I was stupid but..." she continued, getting glossy-eyed.

That's when Andre interjected, "Baby you weren't stupid, you were only in love like you said. I understand perfectly. That's not your fault, you're a woman and most black women love hard like that. Don't beat yourself up over it."

Andre took another sip of Hennessy through his coffee-straw and asked, "So when do you go to court?"

"I have to go to roll call this Tuesday morning but my lawyer says that it could be another six months before my case actually gets heard."

"So this lawyer, what is he doing to try to help you beat the charges?"

"Basically, there's nothing that he can do. If I can't come up with a reasonable explanation for how I bought those things, I could be facing some serious time."

Andre remained silent for a moment, trying to figure out some type of solution to her problem. Then he asked, "So, how much stuff did he actually put in your name?"

"A two-story house, a Range Rover, an Acura TL and a 3 Series BMW", she answered, poignantly.

"Is that it?" Andre asked, minimizing her problem.

That's when Promise lifted her head and asked, "What do you mean?"

Andre took another sip, considering the idea that had suddenly came to mind. After a few more seconds, he said, "I think I know how I can help you to get those charges dropped".

Promise asked him what he had in mind. He nonchalantly replied, "Just give me your lawyer's contact information and I'm gonna take care of it". Since Andre didn't explain exactly how he had planned on going about it, she felt like he might've been running game. She was indeed impressed by the way that he had planned the entire date but this part just seemed too good to be true. Being careful not to insult him, she replied, "Thanks but you don't have to do that".

Promise was really digging Andre and she didn't wanna allow him to ruin their bond by telling an unnecessary lie. She tried to switch the subject and began talking about her next book that she was planning to write. Andre detected that she was skeptical and then he insisted, "Please...let me at least try". She realized that matters couldn't really get much worse so she gave in. "Okay well, if you really wanna help, I'll give you his card when you take me home tonight".

For the remainder of the night, Promise's mood had changed. She had been lied to so many times before, by Murda, that she had major trust issues. She was beginning to feel like this was gonna be their first and last date. She was feeling insecure due to her court situation, like that would prevent her from keeping a decent man like him. Plus, she thought that Andre had just sold her a dream, simply because he didn't know how to come out and tell her that he saw no future in them.

The cruise lasted for another 45 minutes before the boat returned to the pier where they had first boarded. Then Andre retrieved his Jaguar from the valet. For the majority of the ride back to Bowie Promise remained silent, looking out of the passenger's window. Andre recognized that something was troubling her, assuming that it was the fact that he had put her court situation back on her mind. He realized that bringing up that subject was a bad move from the beginning and that it would be wisest not to reiterate on it. He just remained quiet, let the a/c blow, and listened to Musiq Soulchild until they arrived back at her crib.

They arrived at Promise's apartment around 2:00 a.m. Andre walked her to the front door and she stopped to thank him, making it blatant that she wasn't about to invite him inside. "Well...I had a wonderful time tonight. I really needed that. Thank you." That's what her lips said, although her eyes told another story. It felt more like a somber farewell. "The pleasure was all mine," he replied. Realizing that it was late and that she was probably exhausted, he opened his arms to give her a hug goodbye. That's when she forced out a smile and wrapped her arms around his neck. She kissed his cheek as she pulled away.

"Goodnight", said Promise while turning the key to unlock her front door. That's when Andre reminded her, "Promise... the card". "Oh yeah", she replied, having very little enthusiasm. Andre waited patiently at the front door for a couple of minutes until she returned with Mark Nettles' business card in her hand. Then she handed it to him and he returned to his car, disappointed because he didn't receive a goodnight kiss on the lips.

When Andre got into his car, he cursed himself in the mirror, feeling like he had struck out by bringing up Promise's case on their date. When Promise walked into her house, she placed her back on the door as soon as she closed it. She stood there for a moment, feeling embarrassed like she too had struck out. She was really into this guy and deep down, she was hoping that he was gonna be her knight in shiny armor. But, after that night, she was certain that she had turned him away. That's when she got undressed and retired to her bed to get some sleep.

14

CONVINCED

Promise didn't hear a word from Andre until that Wednesday evening when she got off work at Dick's around 8:00. He had left a message in her voicemail, stating that he needed for her to come down to True Life Publishing one day during regular business hours, so that she could sign a few papers concerning her contract. Her work hours on Friday were short, from 12:00 p.m. until 5:00, so she visited him in his office on Friday morning, first quarter. This time, she brought Zaire along with her.

When Promise and Zaire entered Andre's office, he presented her with a blank copy of the author/publisher agreement that she had filled out at Fleming's Prime Steakhouse & Wine Bar. The first thing that she noticed was that the contract had been backdated to three years before they had ever met. Without thinking to question that simple fact, she filled out the contract for the second time. Only this time, Andre had left the spaces that were provided for the signing-bonus amount and the payment method empty.

Just as she was preparing to leave, Andre surprised her. "And, oh yeah", he began, retrieving a sky blue-colored 6 x 9" soft back book from his desk-drawer. Then he continued, "This just came in yesterday, a galley proof for your book. I need your approval before I tell the printer to begin printing your first 10,000 copies". Promise received the book as she became red in the face from excitement. "Wow, it's beautiful", she said, inspecting the cover design that Andre's graphics designer had done. Then she thumbed through the pages to inspect the type-set and the font styles. It didn't take Promise thirty seconds to give her approval. Then she and Andre agreed to hook up later, and Promise returned home.

In the next few weeks, Promise and Andre really started to get close. They began spending lots of time together, dining out and visiting each other almost daily. There was no doubt in Promise's mind that he was seriously into her, she was finally convinced. The first confirmation was when he introduced her to his two daughters, Joy and Secret. And, the second confirmation came when Promise received an unexpected voice message from Mark Nettles, requesting that she reported to his law firm as soon as possible to discuss her status.

When she walked into his office early one Saturday morning, she was slightly nervous because she had no idea of what to expect. Mark seemed excited to see her. "Good morning Ms. Heyward", he greeted, suggesting with his right hand that she took a seat. Then he walked over to his file cabinet, withdrew a manila envelope and returned to his chair.

Andre's accountant had delivered to Mark, a copy of Promise's new author/publisher agreement, as well as Andre's tax reports for the last three years. The tax reports verified that his publishing company grossed over $1,000,000 each year. Mark placed the documents on the desk in front of Promise and said, "Your friend, Mr. Vasquez, gave me a call earlier this week. He said that he's willing to testify on your behalf and tell the courts that he's been paying you in cash for your services at his company. Now...with those being the facts, and him providing legal documentation, as such, showing that his net worth is a couple million, that pretty much gets you off the hook".

Promise just listened as she looked over the author/publisher agreement, noticing that the signing-bonus amount was now $100,000 and that the payment method was by cash. She was starting to feel like all of her problems were over until Mark continued, "However, there's a catch 22. There is no record of you paying any taxes on the money that he paid you, so the courts may just drop the conspiracy and money laundering charges and charge you with tax evasion. That's a lesser charge and I can almost assure you that you'll receive probation for it since you don't have any priors."

Mark was ready and willing to represent her because he knew that winning a high-profiled case like hers would look good on his track record. He figured that he would've made the front page of The *Baltimore Sun* for that, causing his clientele to sky-rocket through the roof. So, it was mutually beneficial for the both of them. Mark knew that Murda was the media's real focal point and that if he could also win his case that would really boost his career. He was an opportunist, just like any other lawyer, and he viewed winning Promise's case like killing two birds with one stone. After studying both of their cases, Mark realized that Promise's guilt was actually the Feds' crux in Murda's case. Once the courts ruled that Murda's house and all of his cars were purchased by Promise with legal money, that would take most of the heat off Murda. He wouldn't look like such a kingpin after all, and the only case that the Feds had against him now rested upon a lousy audiotape.

Mark then explained how Andre had actually helped both her and Murda in their cases. He also said that the $50,000 that the Feds confiscated would have to be returned to her if the conspiracy and money laundry charges were dropped. That news helped to soothe her conscience because she was still feeling guilty about turning Murda's money and his cell phone over to the Feds. Even though she was starting to get over Murda, and more into Andre, she still felt obligated to relay the good news to Murda. That's when she decided to visit him that night. Visitation hours were from 6 p.m. until 9 p.m., so Promise and Zaire arrived at the jail around 7:30.

Murda and Cool were in their cell playing a game of casino when the dorm-officer's voice came yelling through the intercom in their room, "Reed, get dressed, you have a visit". Murda had no idea of who was visiting him and the last person that he had expected to see was Promise. Had he known that she was coming, he would've at least gotten a haircut and a shave.

When Murda walked into his visitation stall, Promise was waiting on the opposite side of the 2" thick soundproof Plexiglas, sitting in a chair with Zaire sitting on her lap. She was wearing her Dick's uniform and Zaire was wearing a Timberland sweat-suit. It had been a couple of months since Zaire had last seen his pops and he didn't seem all that excited to see him then. Promise was expressionless as she watched Murda sit down in his chair, wearing an inmate jumpsuit and a pair of shower-shoes, with a full beard and in desperate need of a tape-up. Even though she noticed that he had picked up some weight, he definitely didn't have that legendary prison glow that she'd expected. He actually looked kinda washed-up to her.

They both picked up their telephones almost simultaneously, and Murda initiated the conversation.

"Wow, so you finally decided to come and check up on a nigga. What's good?"

"I just felt like you probably wanted to see Zaire, plus I need to let you know what's going on with my court situation", she replied.

Murda hadn't spoken to Mark that day so he was expecting for Promise to tell him what he already knew. That's when he said, "Mark already told me that you're facing like 240 months. Don't worry about that though. I already told him that if he doesn't get you off this, he's gonna be maggot food."

Promise wasn't the least bit impressed by his little tough guy act. She knew that if Andre hadn't stepped up, she would've been up shit's creek without a paddle. She began to explain, "Well, I visited Mark this morning. It sounds like my charges are gonna get dropped because I came up with a legitimate explanation for how I bought the house and the cars. Mark said that the Feds were gonna have to give back the money that was in your safe. As soon as they do that, I'll find a way to get it to you. Mark also said that once I was exonerated of the charges, the Feds wouldn't have much of a case against you and you'll have a better chance of winning your trial."

That made Murda's day, and that's when he jumped to conclusions, "Baby I knew that you were gonna come through for me. I didn't doubt for one second that you had my back. Word, this time it's gonna be right. I'm gonna come home, we're gonna get married and move far away from here. This city's for the birds".

Promise dropped her head because she knew that her next statement was about to ruffle his feathers.

When Murda picked up on the vibe, he asked, "Bay, what's all this silent shit?"

That's when she finally decided to just face the music and confess, "Murda, I've moved on and I'm seeing somebody else now".

Murda furrowed his eyebrows, then he gave a wry grin and said, "Oh yeah? Tell me about him".

Promise could tell that he was hurt, fronting on some macho shit. She continued, "Well, I'm sure that you don't know him but he's a nice guy. He listens to me, he respects me, and most of all, he doesn't mind spending time with me".

Murda was certain that she was serious at that point, and the only words that he could come up with were, "Baby, we need to work this shit out because you're tripping right now".

"There is no more 'we'", she said, conclusively.

Ice coated Murda's heart as those words fell from Promise's lips. His ego was crushed after realizing that Promise was no longer wrapped around his finger. Plus, the idea of another man pleasing her better than he did was eating away at him. Still, he strained to produce a smile and asked, "So...what, you love this nigga?"

Promise hesitated for a moment. Then she replied, "I think I do love him".

Murda gave her a look of disbelief and said, "You can't be serious. So...what, did you sleep with him?"

"That's none of your business," she answered.

Murda could tell by the expression on her face that the answer was yes, and that's when his temper erupted. He clutched the telephone tightly in his fist and started blasting on her, "You fuckin' disloyal, gold diggin'-ass bitch. You've got a lot of nerve coming up here with this bullshit! I don't give a fuck who you're fucking because a hoe's gonna be a hoe. But, if I find out that you got another nigga around my son, I'm gonna give you and him a dirt nap!"

Even though the Plexiglas was soundproof, Murda's voice was still loud enough to startle Zaire and to capture the attention of the c.o. who was in the area. Promise felt so disrespected that she hung up the phone and stood up to cut their visit short. That's when Murda also stood, spat on the Plexiglas and hurled the phone up against it as hard as he could. Zaire started crying so Promise picked him up and walked out of the cubicle. Murda's nose was turned up as he watched her leave. The C.O. heard the loud bang when the phone hit the glass so he rushed over, just as Murda was turning around to return to his cell.

"What the hell is going on up here?" asked the officer, noticing the spit that was slowly trickling down the glass. Murda just gave him an ice grill and said, "Man, mind your fuckin' business!" Then he proceeded back to his cell and waited by the door until the dorm-officer pressed the button on the control panel to let him back inside. When he walked in, Cool was sitting on the top bunk, bagging up some weed. Cool noticed that Murda seemed upset so he asked, "Who was that?" "That was that stupid ass bitch, Promise", he replied, reaching for the last dipper that he had sitting in the window sill. Then he smoked it to the head and listened to some tracks on his I-pod to try to mellow out.

Cool finished bagging up just before lights-out, around 11:00, and then he fell asleep. Murda, on the contrary, didn't sleep at all that night. He tossed and turned for hours, imagining another man taking his spot in Promise's life and interacting with Zaire. His pride was hurt and he was worried about what people were gonna think of him if they spotted Promise out in public with another dude while he was in jail. That idea alone probably unsettled him more than the thought of another man actually fucking her. With Murda, his reputation was everything and there was no limit to what he was willing to do to protect it.

Cool and Redrum only had five days left before their bond reconsideration hearings. Shit didn't look very promising for Cool since he had received a letter from his parole officer. He said that he was gonna violate him and revoke his sentence because of his arrest, but his parole hearing was scheduled for a month later. Redrum, on the other hand, was probably gonna get some play in court since Bang Bang was allowed to walk and they were all co-defendants.

Murda began making out a list of things for Redrum to do, just incase he made bail. Murda had made a mental note of the fact that Promise worked at Dick's, after noticing the insignia on her uniform. He wanted Redrum to find out exactly which Dick's she worked at and who she was living with. Then, go as far as to spy on her and follow her until he found out who was this new boyfriend of hers. He had also drawn out a blueprint for Redrum to get the Dru Hill trap back up and running. And finally, he wanted him to find Bang Bang and make sure that he didn't live to testify against Murda on the date of his trial.

Murda wrote out a two-page long kite to Redrum, using hieroglyphics that only a Blood from his set could've decoded. He passed it off to Bloodsport the next time that he came into the pod to deliver the dinner trays. As soon as Redrum read the kite, he shot a kite back to Murda, agreeing to do the job. He was just happy to know that Murda was gonna be posting his bond, plus he had offered to pay him well. Since Redrum was planning to go AWOL, that extra cash would've came in handy and Murda knew that.

Murda was real crafty; one of those types of guys who felt like money could buy anything. The $25,000 that he had offered to pay Redrum was nothing. Before Murda had even written the kite for Redrum, he had made arrangements for the redbone chick, Erica, to suitcase in a half a pound of Kush for him, solely for that purpose. Spark had compressed two quarter pounds to the size of two Snicker bars and she picked them up that Sunday afternoon at the B-Hive. She was supposed to bring in one cutie pie that night when she went to work and the other when she returned to work on Monday night.

15

RAT HUNTER

One week later….
Murda and Cool were in their cell working-out late Friday evening, just before the officer was about to pop the doors open for rec. Cool had finished first so he was getting prepared to take a shower. Murda was still on the floor, in the front-leaning rest position, straining to finish his last 5 push-ups. That's when Bloodsport slid a kite under their door. Murda finished his last set. Then he rose to his feet as he opened the kite to read it. It had been sent from Redrum and it read:

> "Big B's homie. I went up for my bond hearing this morning and the judge gave me a bond for $30,000 surety or $50,000 cash. Here's my government, Richard Gist, so that you can work that out with the bail

>   bondsman. And you already know I got you
>   on that business. B's up!"

Murda hopped into the shower as soon as the door opened. Then he returned to his cell to make a few calls. First, he called his Blood homie named Bloodshot who was a bail bondsman. Bloodshot said that he could get Redrum released on Monday morning but it was gonna cost about three stacks. Then Murda made arrangements for him to pick up the cash from Blood-bath that weekend. When he hung up the phone, he wrote a response to Redrum's kite, letting him know that everything was everything.

Bright and early Monday morning, Redrum was sleeping on his rack when the c.o.'s voice came through the intercom in his cell. "Mr. Gist. Pack up, you're being released". Redrum jumped up and didn't waste any time. He quickly brushed his teeth, dashed some hot water on his face, and pressed the "talk" button on the intercom, "I'm ready". He had a small blue bin with about twenty dollars worth of snacks in it. He told his roommate that he could have them all, as well as the hygiene items that he hadn't used. The only things that he carried home with him were the letters that his girl, Astria, had sent to him since he'd been in there.

Redrum was escorted to the bookings area to receive his property and to be processed out. It had been over 100 days since he'd been arrested and the season had changed. It was now the beginning of summer so he told the booking officer to trash his all-black aviator flight jacket that he was wearing when he got arrested. Then he received his DDTP World outfit and got dressed. After being released, he walked out of the jail, unbeknownst to the fact that Bloodbath was gonna be wait-ing out front for him. He was planning to walk to the Light Rail to catch the train to Astria's crib on Hamberg Street, near downtown. As soon as he walked out of the jail, he heard a horn honk twice. That's when he realized that the sound had came from Bloodbath's candy apple-red Cadillac Escalade which was parallel parked across the street.

Redrum weaved through the traffic and made his way to the truck. When he hopped into the passenger's seat, Bloodbath passed him a blunt of sour diesel that he'd been puffing on.

"How do you feel, Blood?" asked Bloodbath.

"How do I feel? I feel like getting some pussy", he replied.

As Bloodbath merged into the flow of traffic, he began to commend Redrum, "Youngin, that was some real shit that you did by not folding under pressure. Everybody aint built like us".

"I know, family", Redrum chimed in, realizing that he was referring to Bang Bang. That's when Bloodbath grabbed his cell phone out of the cupholder, dialed Murda's cell number, and turned on the speakerphone.

Murda answered the jack in his raspy early-morning voice, "What's bangin'?".

"What's popping five? I'm just calling to let you know that I just picked up Rum. I'm on the way to drop him off with his Ruby Red."

"Alright, give him both packages for me and make sure that you give him my math", Murda replied. "Big B's homie!"

"B's up!" said Murda just before he hung up the phone to finish resting.

Bloodbath placed his cell back in the cup holder, and then he told Redrum to open the glove compartment. Next, he told him to grab a white envelope that was in clear view when he opened it. Redrum could tell from the shape of the print that there was a stack of bills inside. Thats when Bloodbath said, "Count it and make sure its all there", assuming that Redrum and Murda had already discussed the numbers. The envelope was sealed so Redrum ripped it open from the side and withdrew the contents. "Damn, nothing but big heads", Redrum thought out loud, shuffling through the stack of crispy one hundred dollar bills. Then he counted out 25 stacks, ten bills at a time.

Redrum placed the money in his pocket just as they were pulling up in front of his girl's apartment on Hamberg Street. Thats when Bloodbath handed him a small sheet of paper with his and Murda's cell numbers written on it. Then he told him to grab a brown paper-bag from beneath his seat. Without questioning, Redrum grabbed the bag and found a shiny chrome .38 revolver and a box of bullets inside. Redrum knew that every one of those bullets might as well have had Bang Bang's name written on them. Murda preferred that he used a revolver because he knew that the shell casings would remain in the cylinder, unlike any other type of gun. Redrum then concealed the weapon beneath his shirt and proceeded into the house.

Redrum laid up with his girl all morning, then she fixed him a plate of soul food and he took a hot shower. He needed to cop some new gear so he grabbed a couple of stacks and walked to the subway station to catch the train to Mondawmin Mall, aka Murder Mondawmin. Mondawmin got that name in the early 90's after a young squad of wild niggas rode through the mall on bikes and shot it up, killing a few innocent shoppers. When he walked out of the apartment, Astria was in the living-room, parked in front of the computer.

Redrum brainstormed for that entire day, striving to figure out how he was gonna find out which Dick's Promise worked at. He knew that was Murda's primary concern, and that Bang Bang was secondary. By that evening, when he returned to Astria's crib, his only idea was to Google Dick's Sporting Goods in Maryland and jot down the phone numbers to each store. He had planned to call each store and ask for Promise's full name.

He was done shopping at Mondawmin around 6:00 and he arrived back at Astria's pad around 7:15. When he walked inside, he found Astria still parked in front of the computer.

"Bay, I'm gonna need the computer in a few minutes so that I can look something up", said Redrum, walking towards the bedroom to put away his new outfits.

Astria was bugging out, laughing at something that was on the computer screen.

Redrum walked back into the living-room almost ten minutes later. "Damn baby, you're still on that damn computer? What the hell are you doing anyway?" he asked, as he pierced his eyes on the screen.

"I'm just checking my Facebook messages, give me a minute"

"I heard a few niggas behind the g-walls talking about Facebook, what is that shit?"

"It's just an easy way to find old friends and meet new people. Me, I just use it to be nosy and keep up with the joneses"

"So, can you find anybody on there?"

"Anybody who's somebody", she answered, just before laughing at another message that had just appeared in her inbox.

Redrum rubbed his chin and gazed off into the distance, as if a brilliant idea had just came to mind. Then he said, "Before you log out, see if you can find my cousin Promise. I think she married this cat named Mike, so try Promise Heyward".

Unaware of what Redrum was actually up to, Astria typed-in Promise's full name and they both waited patiently for the search results. After a few seconds, Astria said, "This girl is from out of Bowie, is this her?"

Redrum vaguely remembered what she looked like, so he asked, "Is that her only picture?"

"No, she has 47 profile pictures", Astria replied, pulling up the other photos.

Redrum viewed five more photos before realizing that she was definitely the girl that he was looking for. That was because she had posted a picture of Zaire who was a spitting image of Murda. That's when he continued, "Hell yeah that's my cousin, find out what she's doing now".

"If her page is private, I wont be able to", she replied as she attempted to pull up Promise's personal information.

Promise's Facebook page wasn't set to private so Astria was able to access her personal information. Her address and phone number weren't listed but he did learn that she currently lived in Bowie. Her page also revealed that she was employed as a crew manager at Dick's, not disclosing the store's exact location.

Feeling like his findings were of very little help, he was taken aback when Astria said "I thought you said that she was married to somebody named Mike. Right here, it says that she's in a relationship with a man named Andre Vasquez".

Redrum's eyes lit up like Christmas trees,and then he asked, "Can you pull him up too?"

"Yeah, he's in her relationship link", she answered, attempting to pull up Andre's page.

Unfortunately, Andre's page was private. The only things that they were allowed to see were his profile picture and his basic info like where he worked, and his date of birth. When he noticed that Andre was dressed in a suit, Redrum automatically assumed that he was the square-john type. He couldn't wait to call Murda to tell him about the progress that he had made in only a matter of hours since he'd been released. After realizing that he'd found out every drop of information that Facebook had to offer, he told Astria to log out and show him how to use Google.

Once Astria pulled up the Google search engine, she left the room to take a shower while Redrum handled his business. When he googled Dick's Sporting Goods in Maryland, he realized that they had stores in Bel-Air, Glen Burnie, Columbia, Hagerstown, Baltimore, Waldorf, Salisbury and over twenty more locations. It took almost 45 minutes for him to write-down the phone numbers and addresses to each store. Then he shut off the computer and called Murda to relay the news.

Murda was on his cell phone, talking to Winter, when Redrum tried to call, so he didn't answer. That's when Redrum left a message in his voicemail, telling him to return his call as soon as possible. Shortly afterwards, Astria entered the bedroom, dressed in a fuchsia and white laced lingerie set that she had copped from Victoria's Secret. It was only a matter of seconds before Redrum was ripping it off of her and pounding her back out. They fucked for a couple of hours, then they both slept until the next morning.

When Redrum woke up the next morning, his mission was to begin searching for Bang Bang. He knew that it would only be a matter of time before his trial date came up. He was gonna stall the courts by retaining his innocence claim, just to buy more time. As soon as Mark Nettles would've started talking like his time was near, he was gonna get low. He knew that since Murda had paid him in advance, fulfilling his end of the bargain was a prerequisite for him to even think about bouncing. He wanted to get Murda out of the way, get the Dru Hill trap back poppin', then hustle and stack as much bread as he could before it was time for him to skate out of town.

Bang Bang and Redrum were actually pretty close before the bust went down. They both grew up in Upton Druid Apartments on Druid Hill Avenue. They knew each other's families and the whole nine. On the same token, Redrum was really fervid when it came down to Blood protocol and, when he learned that Bang Bang was dropping dimes, all of that friend shit became irrelevant. We're talking about a man who had "Death, Before Dishonor" tatted across his chest and "Blood business is never personal" tatted on his forearm.

In all of the Blood territories, Bang Bang's status was "persona non grata." Redrum knew that finding Bang Bang would be virtually impossible, so he began trying to figure out a way to make Bang Bang come to him. After many hours of brainstorming, the thought occurred to him that his best option would be to use Bang Bang's grandmother as a conduit to get to him. Her name was Nana, and Redrum knew that she was Bang Bang's heart. She too lived in the Druid Hill Park area, in these apartments for the elderly, called Memorial Apartments.

Andre's oldest daughter, Secret, had a birthday that weekend so he threw a private party for her at the Dave and Buster's in Friendship Heights, out in Northwest D.C., not too far from his daughters' neighborhood. Besides his youngest daughter, Joy, he invited Promise, Zaire and a group of Secret's friends from school, both black and white alike. The kids were having so much fun entertaining themselves that they weren't even paying any attention to their chaperons, Andre and Promise. That's when Andre decided to speak, softly, to Promise, concerning her book.

"You know that your books should be arriving this week"

"Oh yeah? That's great", Promise replied, laughing at little Zaire because he was flirting with one of the little girls.

Andre continued, "I'm still gonna have my distributors to send copies of your book to different bookstores in all of the major cities but, this is my first time dealing with this type of problem."

"Problem?", Promise asked.

"You see…usually when my new authors release a book we go on a tour to different cities and do autograph signings at different bookstores. That's how we promote the book and generate sales. We have to do live radio interviews and everything because the books are not gonna sell themselves. Without the right promotion, nobody's gonna know who you are so your books will only be sitting on the shelves and collecting dust. You can't even leave the state because you're on bond. Plus, you have to go to roll call once a week."

That part of the equation came to her as a surprise, and she began to feel embarrassed because she hadn't considered such a no-brainer. Clueless about what to do, she asked Andre for his advice.

Andre sat ponderously for a few seconds, then he answered, "The only thing that I can think of is to talk to Mark Nettles and find out what's it gonna take to speed up the process. He already said that you should beat the case so, I don't understand why he's procrastinating."

Promise nodded her agreement, then replied, "Well, first thing Monday morning, I'm gonna go down to his office and find out what's good because I'm ready to get this chapter of my life behind me."

"That's a good idea bay. As a matter of fact, I'll go with you."

That's when Promise and Andre decided to set all of their book business aside so that they could refocus their attention on the kids. The party went on for about two hours, and then Andre and Promise carried all the kids home in Andre's all-black Ford Excursion.

Monday morning, around 9:00, Andre scooped up Promise and Zaire in his Lambo. He had promised his receptionist that he would be at work around 12:00, that afternoon, so he was pressed for time. They arrived at Mark Nettles' law firm around 10:00. When they all went inside, Mark was standing at the coffee machine, dressed sharply as usual, filling up his coffee mug.

"Ms. Heyward, how are you?", Mark asked.

"I'm fine, and how are you?", she replied.

"Would you two like some coffee? We have cream and sugar but I drink mine cowboy-style."

"No thanks, we're actually in a hurry. I really just dropped in to discuss my status"

"Well...right this way", he said, leading the way to his office down the hall.

When they all took their seats, Andre got straight down to business. He had more knowledge about the legal process from his past experiences, so he initiated the conversation, "So, how certain are you that my statement and my tax reports are gonna get her off the hook?"

Realizing that Andre definitely meant business, Mark wiped the silly smile from his face and tried to look as serious as possible. "Sir, I'm about 99.9% sure that this is gonna work."

"Well, what's the hold up? Why can't we request a speedy trial?"

Mark didn't answer right away, giving Andre an inkling that the whole 99.9% rap was some bullshit. Then he began, "I could put in a motion for a speedy trial."

"And when can you get us in front of a judge?", Andre interjected.

"Well, if the judge grants her a speedy trial, he has six months to get her in court or he will have to throw her case out. If that's what you want me to do, then I'll get on it right away."

16

THE WATCHER

M urda didn't return Redrum's call until around 11:00 a.m., that following Thursday. He was lying alongside Astria in bed at the time.

"What's poppin?" Redrum answered, after noticing that Murda was the person who was calling.

Then he walked out of the room so that they could discuss their business privately.

"Yeah, I'm back. I thought that you were never gonna call".

"You know how busy I am. Even in jail it still feels like there aren't enough hours in the day"

"Yeah, I know how you get down. If it don't make dollars, it don't make sense", Redrum added, pulling Murda's dick.

Redrum continued, "I found out who your wifey is dealing with".

"Oh word, what's up wit 'em?"

"Just some square-john, bamma-ass nigga named Andre Vasquez. I aint sure where he's from but he works at this spot called True Life Publishing or some shit. I looked it up online and all I found was a P.O. Box address. But, I'm on it. That's on Blood"

"True, and did you find out where Promise is living at?"

"Give me a week young, I got you"

"Bet that up. What about that pussy-ass nigga Melvin?"

"Who?"

"Melvin, I'm not calling that nigga Bang Bang"

"Oh!, I was thinking about swinging by his grandmother's crib over on McMechen Street. If worse came to worst, I'd body that old bitch, then come through and wet his ass up at the funeral", Redrum blurted out, using the fact that Bang Bang had ratted as a rationale for killing the innocent woman.

Murda replied, "That won't be necessary homie, I think that I have a better idea. Do you remember the little white bitch that he used to have with him a few years ago?"

"Which one? That's all that nigga used to fuck with", Redrum answered sarcastically.

"The one that used to drive him around all the time in that white Camry that looked like Bloodbath's shorty's shit"

"Oh, you're talking about Chrissy, the little chick from out of Landover. Yeah, she had that nigga's head fucked up when she left him"

"I remember. He slapped her or some shit, right?"

"Yeah, he smacked her, and then she left his ass stinking. That's when he fell off and started fucking with that shiesty ass bitch Keisha"

"Oh, she's shiesty? I gave her like 500 to put on that nigga's books when he was in here"

"Oh, you'd better believe...she spent that shit"

"Word?"

"Without a doubt in my mind she spent it."

Realizing that the C.O. was about to do his 11:30 head-count, Murda decided to cut their conversation short, "Ayo bruh, let me make a few phone calls, I'll get back at you on this. In the meantime, keep posting and find out what's up with Promise and this Vasquez cat".

"I got you family, hold your head"

"Yea, all the time."

The officer did his count and, subsequently, Murda called Winter on her cell phone. Over the past couple of weeks, they had been conversing regularly and Murda was slowly making his way back in her good graces. She had the capacity in her heart to forgive Murda, unlike Promise. They had been discussing his court situation, and Winter had already put it out there that she was willing to help him, however she could. He was gassing her up to believe that they were gonna get married when he got released. She was all for it, whether it was because of the sex or the simple fact that she'd became accustomed to sitting in the lap of luxury. Whatever the case was, Murda was playing her like a fiddle because his heart was truly with Promise.

The phone call lasted for almost one hour. Besides the fact that Cool was trying to get some sleep, Murda kept his voice down for the sake of eavesdropping vent-partners. It took almost 45 minutes for Murda to come up with a plan to lure Bang Bang in. That was with the help of Winter, of course, as she gave her input about the situation. Once Murda felt like Winter thoroughly understood her role in the whole ordeal, he ended their conversation to begin mobilizing everyone else that he had involved in his scheme.

Meanwhile, Redrum was at Astria's crib, calling every Dick's Sporting Goods store on his list. Feeling like almost every effort was made, Redrum was down to his last three stores before he finally got lucky.

That's when he called the store located inside of the Glen Burnie Mall, and a female answered, "Dick's Sporting Goods, how may I direct your call?"

"Yes, may I speak to Ms. Promise Heyward please?" asked Redrum, trying to sound as sophisticated as possible.

The woman replied, "I'm sorry sir but Promise doesn't come in until 5:00 this evening. May I take a message?"

"No thanks. I'll just try back later. Thanks again"

"You're welcome sir, and have a nice day"

"You too", Redrum replied, just before hanging up the phone.

Using his faculty of reasoning, Redrum figured that Promise's work hours were from 5:00 until closing, since the Glen Burnie Mall closed at 11:00. In all of the 26 years that he'd been living in Maryland, he didn't know shit about Glen Burnie. He didn't know how far it was, nor which highway he needed to take to get there. Furthermore, he didn't have a driver's license or a car to drive. That's when he decided to call up one of his old partners named Walt, who was originally from Dru Hill. Walt had left Baltimore after he graduated from high school, and he moved out to Glen Burnie with this chick that he had married from out there.

Walt was all amped when he realized that Redrum was calling his phone. Most niggas from Dru Hill started treating him like his ghetto-pass had been revoked ever since he got married and left the hood. Back in the days, Walt was just a pushover who Redrum and his homies used to use for rides to go and fuck bitches or make drops. He always had cars, ever since high school and his family always seemed more well off than the typical families around Dru Hill. Redrum and his crew would practically kidnap him and hold him hostage for days at a time.

"What's up Richard?" asked Walt, calling Redrum by his government name that he remembered from high school, before he became Blood.

"What's poppin Walt? How's life been treating you out there in the county?"

"I can't complain. What's going on though?"

Redrum tried to be very particular about his diction, being careful not to sound too conspicuous. He knew that if Walt detected that there was any funny business, he would've made up any little lame excuse for why he couldn't take part in whatever it was that he wanted him to do.

Redrum answered, "Basically, I need to meet someone at the Glen Burnie Mall tonight but I don't know how to get there. Since you live in the town, I was wondering if I could fill up your tank and have you to pick me up, take me there and bring me back".

Off top, Walt flashed back to the days when Redrum used to have him riding dirty with drugs and guns, against his own will. Careful not to sound like a bitch, he said, "I can't help you tonight because I have to work at the library".

"And, where is the library at?"

"The library is on Ritchie Highway, the same street as the mall, about one mile away. But, by the time that I knock off, the mall will be closed"

"Oh word? What time do you knock off?" "The library closes at 9:00 but I'm not allowed to leave until ten."

Walt suggested, "Why don't you just catch the Light Rail out here and I'll just pick you up from the mall when I get off?"

Walt was hoping that Redrum would've said nevermind but, little did he realize, that would've been perfect timing. He realized that he had put his own foot in his mouth when Redrum asked, "Ok, so, once I get off the train, then where do I go?"

Walt was left with no other option but to give Redrum the instructions on how to find the mall. Then Walt ended their conversation, assuring him that he would be waiting in the Dick's parking lot, in an all-white Dodge Charger on deuces.

Redrum didn't want to arrive at the mall too early and end up loitering around. He waited until around 8:00 to walk to the Light Rail stop on Hamberg Street, just a few blocks away from Astria's crib. The only things that he carried along with him were the .38 revolver that he had gotten from Bloodbath, his cell phone, and some pocket change, just incase Walt got shook and decided to stand him up.

Redrum had to take the Light Rail to a stop called Patapsco, just off of Ritchie Highway, and basically in Glen Burnie. The ride was approximately thirty minutes long. That particular Light Rail stop had a MTA bus stop in the parking lot. Redrum waited for another twenty minutes until his bus arrived, mall bound.

It was roughly 9:15 when he arrived at the mall. The mall was relatively small in comparison to malls like the Columbia Mall or Mondawmin. When he walked inside, he noticed that the mall practically looked deserted, having only a few shoppers straggling, doing their last minute shopping before the mall closed. His first stop was at the Dick's store. He spotted Promise almost immediately, servicing one of the customers. She was rocking the same hair-style that she had worn on her Facebook profile picture. Even in her uniform, she looked so beautiful that Redrum almost found himself doting over her. He knew that to even entertain that thought would've gotten his ass sent to the gallows, so he snapped out of it quick-like.

Promise didn't know Redrum, neither did she notice him watching her from a distance. After seeing what she looked like in person, Redrum decided to play the mall and to check out a few other stores before the mall closed. Around 10:00, he decided to call Walt and make sure that everything was still going according to plan. When Walt answered, Redrum told him to text him whenever he arrived in the parking lot and to try to park as close as he could to Dick's front entrance. Walt agreed, preparing him that he would be leaving shortly.

Around 10:45, the mall announcement came over the intercom, reverberating through the entire mall, "The mall will be closing in ten minutes...the mall will be closing in ten minutes". Almost simultaneously, Redrum received a text from Walt, letting him know that he was already in the parking lot in front of Dick's. That's when he walked outside to his car and took a seat in the passenger's seat.

"What's poppin' my ninja?" asked Redrum, slapping Walt's palm as hard as he could.

Walt jerked back his hand and said, "gaaaaad damn!"

"Nigga that shit didn't hurt. I see you're still sensitive than a muthafucka."

Walt was about to put the key in the ignition when Redrum stopped him, "No, I'm still waiting for my people to get off. Just chill, they'll be out in a second".

Walt sighed, and then he looked toward the Dick's entrance door. In his mind, he was thinking, "Here we go again. This nigga Richard is still on his same old bullshit."

Walt turned back the key so that they could listen to some music while they were waiting. Then Redrum started asking him questions about his square-ass lifestyle in the suburbs, pretending to really be interested. After almost thirty minutes, a security guard opened the door and a group of people walked out of the mall, both customers and employees alike. They were coming out in rapid succession so Redrum beamed in to make sure that Promise wasn't in the crowd. A few seconds later, a second group of people came out, some dressed in Dick's uniforms. It only took a few seconds for him to spot Promise. She had fallen back like she was waiting for someone to pick her up from the front entrance, while most of the others continued to their cars.

"There she is", Redrum thought out loud, remaining seated. Promise then reached into the Hermes clutch bag that she was carrying, and withdrew her cell phone to make a call.

"Well, aren't you gonna go talk to her?" asked Walt, starting to suspect that Redrum was up to something.

"Nah...chill", Redrum replied, paying close attention to Promise's every move.

After a couple of minutes, Andre's red and silver Lamborghini pulled up in front of her and she hopped inside.

"Ayo, follow that car homie"

"What?!", Walt exclaimed.

"Just drive muthafucka! I'm not about to do shit...wit' your scary ass."

Walt then gave another bitch-like sigh, turned on the headlights and started the car. Andre was about to turn right onto Ritchie Highway, going into the direction of Interstate 95. Walt followed in pursuit with a stomach full of butterflies, wondering what he had gotten himself caught up in. As they traveled down Ritchie Highway, Redrum made sure that Walt remained at least two cars behind them so that they wouldn't realize that they were being followed.

After almost two miles, Andre veered off onto Interstate 95 and Walt followed his lead, still keeping a reasonable distance between them. "Man, I've gotta get home to my wife Richard. This car could be on the way to Jersey as far as we know", said Walt. Redrum just gave him a look of disgust. Then he pulled the .38 from his pocket, placed it in his lap and threatened, "Man, if you don't shut the fuck up and drive....". Right then, Walt got in total compliance. He planted his back flat up against his chair and drove like he was going on a family vacation.

He didn't know where they were going but Walt felt somewhat relieved when Andre turned off on the Bowie exit. Almost five minutes later, he and Promise turned into an apartment complex on English Oaks Avenue, called Heather Ridge Apartments. There was a convenient amount of traffic filtering in and out of the complex, so Redrum told Walt to turn into the complex and park close enough for him to see which apartment they were gonna walk into.

Walt and Redrum waited as Promise and Andre stepped out of the car. That's when Andre opened his back door to pick up Zaire and carry him inside. He had been sleeping in the backseat. Then they walked into Promise's apartment. Redrum couldn't make out the apartment number on the door from where they were parked at. Once they were inside and a few lights had been turned on in the apartment, Redrum told Walt to drive up closer to the door so that he could see the apartment number. Redrum didn't waste any time. Before they even left the parking lot, he began texting a message to Murda's cell phone that read:

> "*Promise and dude are living together in Bowie, in Heather Ridge Apartments, apartment 6d. The nigga she's fuckin' with is pushing a Lamb, with a customized license tag that says TLP-000. And, can you believe this bitch-ass nigga was carrying your son?*"

17

THE SET-UP

Murda refused to remove the cataracts of denial from his eyes, convincing himself that Promise still belonged to him. The latter part of Redrum's message struck him like a lightning bolt to the chest, but that was only more fuel for his fire. That entire week, Murda was restless, thirsting for Bang Bang's blood and making calls to deploy every accomplice who was to be involved in his murder.

Redrum didn't receive a reply from Murda until that following Thursday evening. Murda sent him a text message, alerting him that he had given his cell phone number to Winter and that she would be calling him later on that night. Murda wanted Redrum to hook up with Winter early on Friday morning so that he could show her where Bang Bang's grandmother, Nana, lived. Redrum knew that Astria would've blown up on him if Winter picked him up from her apartment. So, the next morning, he met Winter at Camden Yards by the Orioles' stadium.

Winter was driving her silver Nissan Altima. She had her youngest son, Josiah, with her, strapped down in a car seat in the backseat. The child was still knocked out. Redrum didn't know exactly what it was that Winter was about to do, but what he did know was that he wasn't in any position to question Murda's authority. Therefore, he just did everything that he was told and he told Winter everything that she needed to know.

When they arrived at Memorial Apartments, Winter parked her car and said to Redrum, "Well...here goes nothing". Then she grabbed Josiah from the backseat and proceeded to Nana's apartment, seemingly confident that she was about to be successful in her undertaking. Nana answered the door after Winter had knocked at least six times. She was wearing a red plaid bathrobe, some black leather bedroom slippers, and one of those head-scarves like Aunt Jemina used to wear.

"May I help you?" Nana asked. "How are you doing ma'am, is Melvin home?"

"Melvin doesn't live here anymore honey", Nana answered, looking curiously at the mulatto child who was sound asleep with his head resting on Winter's shoulder.

When she picked up on the disturbed expression on Winter's face, Nana continued, "Is something wrong child?"

"I don't know if you remember me but I used to date your grandson a few years ago, he brought me by here a few times..."

Nana noticed one of her nosey neighbors named Ms. Anne, standing in her doorway and eavesdropping on their conversation. That's when Nana cut her off at midsentence and insisted, "We can talk inside, come on in." Once inside, they both sat down at the kitchen table and Nana asked, "What was your name again?"

"Chrissy", she replied.

"I really need to talk to Melvin if you can make that possible. When we lost contact over two years ago, I was pregnant with his child and he didn't know it. I call him M.J., for Melvin junior", she continued, indicating Josiah.

Considering Bang Bang's life-long affinity for white girls, Nana found Winter's story to sound very plausible.

Bang Bang had not visited Nana in over two months but he called her frequently from his cell phone. She knew that he was in some type of trouble, remembering how he emphasized that she didn't disclose his phone number to anyone. She didn't even know his whereabouts, only that he was calling from an 804 area code.

"Well baby, I really don't know how to get in contact with Melvin unless he calls or comes by. I can give him your number whenever he does", said Nana.

"That would be great", said Winter, retrieving an ink pen and an old receipt from her purse.

Murda had told Winter to buy a prepaid cell phone and to record the name Chrissy on the standard voicemail greeting. It was that phone's number that Winter wrote down on the back of the receipt.

Nana received the number, then placed the receipt behind a magnet on the refrigerator door, assuring Winter that she would not forget to relay the message.

That's when Winter rose to her feet and prepared to leave, "Alright well, I'm not gonna hold you up any longer. Thank you so much for all of your help".

"You're fine, I wasn't busy at all."

"Well, I need to hurry up and get this boy to day care, then I have to be at work by 12:00. I have to drive all the way back to Landover."

That's when Nana also rose to her feet and escorted Winter to the door.

When it was all said and done, Winter pranced back to her car, feeling proud like she knew that she had just performed like a pro. Now, it was just a matter of waiting for Bang Bang to bite the bait.

Redrum spent the remainder of that week getting Murda's crack spot in Dru Hill Projects cranked back up. Murda realized that his mistake the first time was serving the fiends out of the same apartment that they were cooking and bottling the cracks up in, so he devised a new plan. This plan was a lot more organized, having a chain of command and everything. Bloodbath had been appointed as the captain, Redrum was lieutenant and they had a few of their younger Blood homies playing the roles of the private soldiers. Murda had Redrum to set up shop in this ex-smoker named Clareese's crib, on the third floor.

Bloodbath's responsibility was to deliver the bricks, the baking soda, the B12, and the vials to Redrum at Clareese's apartment. Redrum's job was to monitor Clareese while she cooked up the coke, and help her bottle the cracks up in the vials. The tenants' mailboxes were located on the first floor in the hallway, and that was where the product was gonna be stashed at. The key holder was this kid named Infrared. He and five other guys had to work a 7 a.m. to 7 p.m. shift, seven days a week, serving fiends in the vestibule of the building. They were ordered to never keep any drugs in their possession, and to only get the work out of the mailboxes after the cash was put into their hands. If the Feds ever decided to run up in the building, they would only find a mailbox key, which they would most likely overlook in their rampant search for drugs. There were two guns stashed in the mailboxes as well.

Once Clareese and Redrum had whipped up the first batch and bottled it all up, it was time to start back booming. Murda had chosen Infrared because he knew that he was a young thirsty nigga who had been hustling around Dru Hill for years. He knew almost every junkie in the area.

Eversince the Dru Hill raid, all of the smokers had been longing for that good shit that Murda used to keep their neighborhood flooded with. That shit was like straight drop compared to what they'd been smoking since the jump-outs swept through and shut everything down. Some smokers even traveled as far as Murda's spots in Westport and Park Heights just to get a good blast. One thing about Dru Hill, sound traveled fast whenever the word got out that some good dope was floating around. If you had it, all you had to do was tell the right smoker and the news would surely spread like mustard. Infrared knew the perfect person to choose for his messenger, this crack head named Crumb who lived on the second floor.

Crumb was this funny-looking black guy with only like two teeth left in his grill and a few patches of hair on his head. He always walked around with a camouflage army fatigue jacket on, even in the summertime. He got his name from the young hustlers around the projects because he used to always walk around, begging, "Can I get a crumb?" referring to the leftover shakes in their packs.

It was Friday morning when Infrared arrived at Crumb's door, bright and early. The only thing that he had to say was, "Crumb, you already know that I'm gonna take care of you. Let everybody know that I'm giving out testers on the park at 12:00". Then he dropped three vials in his palm and proceeded back to his crib.

When Infrared arrived on Dru Hill Park at 12:00, more than 50 smokers were scattered all over the park, lying in wait for Infrared to come through and make it rain. It looked like a crack house grand opening or some shit. As soon as they spotted him approaching, they all drew in towards him like a pride of starving lions. Both of his hands were filled with $20 crack vials. Without even having to say one word, Infrared walked into the crowd and tossed both handfuls into the air. Then he turned to walk away before they even hit the ground, without looking back one time. That's when everyone started scrambling, pushing and shoving each other to get to the vials that were now scattered all over the ground.

Within four days, Infrared and his team had moved an entire brick in twenty dollar pieces. If they would've kept shop opened 24/7, they would've moved it a lot sooner. Dru Hill was practically a goldmine for anybody who was selling hard drugs, everything from ready rock to heroin. Redrum's determined idea was to stack another 100k, on top of the $24,000 that he already had stashed away at Astria's crib. Then he'd planned to relocate down south to Winston-Salem, North Carolina. That's where Astria was originally from, and she still had some family living there.

Redrum was averaging almost two grand a day, Bloodbath made a little more, and Infrared and his partners made anywhere between seven and eight hundred dollars a day. Everybody was eating, even though all of the real money was going to Murda. Being at the helm, he more than doubled what he spent on each key in a matter of days, simply by sitting in his cell, making a few phone calls and directing traffic.

It was around 11:30 one Wednesday night when Redrum returned to Astria's crib, after a long day in the trap. Even though trap hours were from 7 to 7, he was always the last person to leave. At the end of each day, he had to tally up the cash, count up the leftover crack vials, then hit off Infrared and his two partners. Bloodbath always scooped him up when he was done, so that he could collect his and Murda's portion of the cash. Then he would drop him off at his rest.

When he walked into the apartment on this particular Wednesday night, Astria was asleep in bed so he walked directly to the closet to stash his money in his safe. As he was cracking the code on the safe, he felt his cell phone vibrating in his pants-pocket. When he answered it, it was Murda calling to inform him that a Nine was scheduled for the following day at the B-Hive. He, Bloodbath, Spark and a handful of other Bloods were mandated to be there at 1:30 that Thursday afternoon. Murda never really expounded on what the meeting was gonna be about.

Bang Bang had finally called the cellphone number that Winter had given to his grandmother, Nana. No one besides Nana had that number so Winter knew that the first caller would've been Bang Bang. When his call came through around 9:30 that Wednesday night, Winter allowed the phone to ring until the voicemail greeting came on. Thats what Murda had instructed her to do, so that Bang Bang would hear the name Chrissy in the standard greeting. When Bang Bang heard that the voice was that of a white female, he automatically fell for it. He hadn't heard Chrissy's actual voice in over two years. Winter waited patiently by the phone for Bang Bang to call again. Bang Bang, on the other hand, was hesitating. Now feeling like he was about to get another shot at getting back with Chrissy, he was rehearsing his lines and trying to get his thoughts together about what he was gonna say. In the few months that he'd been in Newport News, so far, he'd yet to find another woman who was tantamount to Chrissy, at least not in his eyes.

When he finally summoned the courage to call again, it was almost 10:30. That's when Winter answered after the second ring, "Hello....Hello!" Bang Bang felt sorta nervy in the beginning but he kept his cool and said, "Chrissy, what's good?" "Hello!" Winter yelled once again, pretending not to have heard what he said. Then she sucked her teeth and hung up the phone.

Bang Bang was befuddled at first, then he rationalized that she must've had bad reception. That's when he decided to send her a text message, letting her know that he was the person calling. Before he could finish texting her, a notification popped up on his screen, letting him know that he had an incoming text message. When he realized that the message had been sent from the same number that he was texting, he deleted his own message and opened Winter's. It read, "Who is this? I dropped my phone in my dishwater today and unfortunately, I can't hear anyone. lol :)."

Murda had told her to do it that way because he wasn't sure whether Chrissy used to call him by Bang Bang or Melvin. In a couple of seconds, he replied, "This is Bang Bang, long time no hear from, lol". Thats when Winter gave another Oscar award-winning performance. Trading text messages back and forth, Winter had that nigga's nose wide open. She stroked his ego, saying how she never stopped loving him, how she missed him and that she especially missed his black dick inside of her. She used the Jedi mind trick, avoiding any topics that would've given her away.

By the end of their conversation, he had revealed to her that he was currently living in Newport News and that he had officially renounced himself as a Blood. He had also agreed to pay her a visit that following Sunday evening at an address that Murda had told her to give to him, 1217 West Eighth Street in Pasadena, Maryland. Winter forwarded each text message to Murda just before she went to bed that night.

The address in Pasadena belonged to one of Bloodbath's concubines named Melanie. The neighborhood was type bourgeois, and predominately white. Melanie's house was a blue and white two-story house with a fence all around it and a huge backyard. The houses on that block were widely dispersed and the neighbors usually minded their own business.

Bloodbath picked up Redrum in his Escalade around 12:00 Thursday afternoon; and then they rode to the B-Hive together, linking up with Spark and a few others. Bloodbath had the entire blueprint to their plan, and it was incumbent upon him to make sure that all of the others understood their positions and were available at the designated time of execution. The meeting lasted for over an hour, and then everyone went their separate ways. Bloodbath dropped Redrum back off in the projects to make sure that everything was running smoothly.

Melanie had left Bloodbath with the keys to her crib while she went out of town to visit her grandparents in Roxbury, Massachusetts. She wasn't expected to return until the following Wednesday. Bang Bang had texted Winter and said that he would be taking the Greyhound bus to the Baltimore bus terminal, downtown. Then he was gonna catch a hack or a cab to Pasadena. He assured her that he would be there around 5:00 or 6:00, Sunday evening.

When Sunday came around, everybody arrived at Melanie's house early in the afternoon. Bloodbath, Redrum and three other Bloods arrived in Bloodbath's main lady's white Toyota Camry. Spark drove his brand new big-body Dodge Ram truck, with some rope and a 10 X 12' roll of carpet on the bed of the truck. He parked the truck in the backyard. Winter parked her Altima outside of the fence, then she went inside with all of Murda's Blood homies. They all made sure that she felt comfortable around them, praising Murda and telling her how much they respected him.

For the entire time, Winter was under the impression that she was setting Bang Bang up to get beaten for turning his back on the Bloods. She had no idea that she was actually making herself an accessory to his murder, especially since the Bloods were acting so calm and casual about everything. The plan was that, whenever Bang Bang arrived in his cab, all she had to do was walk out of the house, say a few lines to Bang Bang, then hop in her car and leave.

Everybody was chilling in the living room with the blinds opened so that they would have a view of the street whenever Bang Bang's cab pulled up. And, like clockwork, around 5:15, a small black Mitsubishi Galant stopped in the middle of the street, directly in front of Melanie's house. When Bloodbath noticed the parked car, he peeked through the blinds and spotted Bang Bang paying the hack. That's when Winter grabbed her keys to leave and all of the men hid themselves in other rooms to wait for their cue. When Bang Bang hopped out of the car, the first thing that he noticed was the white Camry parked inside of the fence. He laughed to himself, remembering the many nights that he used to fuck Chrissy's brains out in her backseat. As he was entering the fence, he looked around to make sure that there weren't any dogs in the yard. His palm was clutching the small .22 Dillinger that was in his pocket. Simultaneously, Winter was walking out of the house, closing the screen door and leaving the wooden door opened.

"You must be Bang Bang", said Winter, walking towards her car.

Bang Bang sized her up, then he replied, "Yeah, how you doin'?".

"I'm fine. My cousin Chrissy told me so much about you. She's inside taking a shower so just go on in and make yourself at home. And, could you close the door when you go in? I left the A/C on and I don't want all of the air to get out."

The sound of the front door closing was the Bloods' cue. By the time that Bang Bang approached the porch, he realized that there were no dogs around so he totally dropped his guard. When he opened the screen door, the first sounds that he noticed were the soft sound of music playing and running shower water coming from the bathroom. When he didn't spot anyone else in the house, he waved goodbye to Winter, and shut the front door.

As soon as he turned around to take a seat, he was staring down the barrel of a 12 gauge Mossberg pump. Bloodbath cocked it back and warned, "If you move, I'll blow your fuckin' head off!" Bang Bang almost shitted on himself, especially when he noticed all of the other Bloods emerging. Redrum immediately walked over to pat him down. When he found the .22 in his pocket, he smacked blood out of his mouth with it, then three of the other Bloods snatched him up and forced him into the bathroom. That's when Bloodbath trained the barrel on the back of his dome, just incase he made any sudden moves.

When they all entered the bathroom, a throwback Biggie song was playing on the radio and the shower water had almost filled the bathtub up to the rim. Before Bang Bang even got the opportunity to beg for mercy, Bloodbath struck him in the back of the head with the butt of the rifle, knocking him unconscious. Bloodbath knew that the gunshots would've probably alarmed the neighbors so he ordered the others to lift him up and drown him in the bathtub.

The water must've woke him up because, after almost thirty seconds of being submerged, he realized that he was being drowned and began kicking and fighting for his life. Water was splashing everywhere and Redrum had to turn up the music to muffle Bang Bang's screams. After a few more seconds, Redrum grew impatient; realizing that drowning him could take all night. Thats when he told all of the other Bloods to back away from the tub. When they did, Bang Bang raised his head out of the water and started gasping for air. That's when Redrum said, "You niggas are taking too long". Then he grabbed Melanie's boom box and dropped it into the water.

Instantly, the water began to electrocute him, sending thousands of volts through his body. Redrum and all of the others even covered their mouths, shocked at the sight of him convulsing from the high voltage. He began drooling, his eyes rolled in the back of his head, and his muscles were starting to lock up on him. After almost forty seconds, a loud explosion sounded and the entire house went dark. Redrum tried to flick the light switch back on, realizing that the radio had knocked out all of the electricity.

Redrum pulled his lighter from his pocket, struck it, and noticed that Bang Bang's head was still underwater and he wasn't moving. That's when Bloodbath unplugged the radio from the outlet and hurried down the hallway to flip the circuit breaker back on. When he returned to the bathroom with all of the others, they were all certain that Bang Bang was dead. His eyes were still opened under the water, and there were no oxygen bubbles rising to the surface.

Bloodbath pulled the stopper out of the drain, then he told Spark and one of the others to grab the roll of carpet from the bed of Spark's truck. When they returned inside with the carpet, they spread it out on the living room floor. Then they stripped Bang Bang completely naked, rolled his stiffening body up in the carpet and tied the rope around it. Spark and Redrum carried the body outside and placed it on the bed of the truck. Bloodbath bagged up Bang Bang's clothes and his cell phone, then he put them in the trunk of the Camry. Then they all got in the car and waited until Spark pulled out first.

Spark had to drive the body all the way out to his partner Black's crib in Jessup, and Bloodbath followed closely behind him so that the cops wouldn't be able to pull him over. Black's crib was in a secluded area, almost five minutes outside of the city limits. Once they arrived there, Spark and two of the other Bloods unloaded the body, then carried it into the back-yard where Black had a pit bull kennel. Black had deliberately starved a few of the dogs for that entire weekend.

When they all walked into the backyard, the dogs were barking ferociously, standing on their hind legs and trying to break their chains to get at them. That's when they laid the carpet roll down on the ground, untied the ropes, and rolled out the carpet to uncover the body. Redrum grabbed Bang Bang by both of his wrists and Spark grabbed him by both of his ankles. Then, on the count of three, they tossed his body into the reach of Black's two most ferocious pits, Beast and Pyscho . As soon as his body touched the ground, the dogs began tearing him to pieces, leaving Bang Bang's family without anything but a mental recall of him. The Bloods' stomachs churned and two of them vomited at the sight of it all. Then they all prepared to leave, knowing that by morning time Bang Bang would be nothing more than a bloodstain on the dirt. Bloodbath called Murda's cell phone as soon as he dropped everyone off and returned home. Murda had been biting his fingernails and waiting nervously for him to call, hoping that everything had ran smoothly. Murda had already spoken to Winter so he knew that Bloodbath and the fellas already had Bang Bang in their restraint.

As soon as Murda noticed Bloodbath's number on his cell phone he answered it before the second ring, "What's poppin'?" Without hesitation, Bloodbath informed him, "Mission complete homie, that nigga's fertilizer now". Murda wiped the sweat bullets from his forehead, and then he told Bloodbath that he would hit him up on the following day.

18

THE VERDICT

5 months later...

"Mr. Nettles, if you'll bring Ms. Heyward to the stand. And, District Attorney McWhite, you are recognized," said Judge Adams.

Promise walked slowly to the stand due to the extra weight that she was carrying, for she was in the second trimester of her pregnancy. She was 5 1/2 months pregnant with Andre's first son. It was warm outside on this particular day so she was wearing a white maternity-style sundress, and a pair of Giuseppe Zanotti sandals.

When Promise arrived on the stand, she remained standing, frequently looking at Andre who was sitting at Mark Nettles' table.

Mr. McWhite asked, "May it please the court?"

The judge nodded his approval, and Mr. McWhite continued, "This is the case against Promise Heyward, indictment number 01-389. She has been indicted for conspiracy and money laundering. Your honor, she is pleading not guilty to count one and count two of this indictment". Mark Nettles had returned to his chair and was sitting alongside Andre.

Judge Adams looked at Mr. Nettles and asked him, "Do you represent Ms. Heyward?"

"Yes, your honor," he replied.

"And have you explained to her the offenses of conspiracy and money laundry, the elements of these offenses, potential defenses, and her constitutional rights?"

"Yes, your honor" "Does she understand these things?" "Yes, your honor" "And, how does she wish to plead?"

"Not Guilty, your honor."

The judge, the attorney general and the three arresting federal agents all looked at Promise, surprised that she had the guts to try to challenge them, knowing that the Feds had a 99% conviction rate. They all wondered what possible defense she could've had, considering all of the unaccounted property, plus the $50,000 that was seized at the time of her arrest. They were certain that her case was gonna be open-and-shut, and had planned to throw the book at her just for wasting the federal government's time and money on having to pay for the jurors and other court expenses.

Judge Adams looked at Mark Nettles and asked, "Mr. Nettles, does your client understand that these are very serious offenses and that if she's found guilty, she's subjected to 240 months in prison?" "Yes, your honor", Mark replied. "And she understands all of the collateral consequences thereof?" "Yes, your honor." Judge Adams then gave Promise a look that read, "You're making a terrible mistake". Then he said to Mark, "Alright. Let's place Ms. Heyward under oath, if we could".

Promise was nervous as hell. Her child was kicking inside of her stomach and her heart must've been beating at one thousand beats per second. When Promise looked at Zaire, Xena, and Antiwan, who were sitting in the courtroom, she noticed that Xena seemed just as nervous as she was. Promise placed her left hand on the Holy Bible, raised her right hand and was duly sworn. Then she explained that she was fully coherent and not under the influence of any drugs or alcohol.

D.A. McWhite looked towards the jury and began summarizing the facts from all of the records that he had. As he was giving his account of the incident, he walked over to the jurors and handed one of them a stack of photos, insisting that he passed them to the other jurors when he was done looking at them. He also gave an identical stack of photos to Judge Adams. They were pictures of the house, all of the cars and the $50,000 that had been seized. Promise remained silent as the D.A. villainized her to the courts, depicting her as one of the ring leaders in a major drug ring. You would've thought that Promise was Lady Heroin, the way that Mr. McWhite was carrying on. The only positive thing that he had to say was that Promise had no prior arrests, nor convictions. As Mr. McWhite was about to close his argument, he mentioned one of Promise's arresting officers, Agent Burroughs. That's when the judge looked at the agent and asked, "Agent Burroughs?"

Agent Burroughs stood, "Your honor, I just wanted to add that the notorious Joseph Reed was apprehended from that same residence just a couple of months prior to her arrest. He was charged with distribution of cocaine in the amount of an entire kilo. We've done a thorough investigation as well as an F.D.I.C check, but were unable to find any record of the defendant being employed during the times that the properties were purchased. We believe that they were bought with Mr.

Reed's illegal drug money." Burroughs paused to add appropriate gravity to the announcement.

McWhite then added his two cents, "And, your honor, I just wanted to add that the cocaine that was procured was packaged in the same packaging as the coke that was seized in the Druid Hill bust earlier this year, giving us reason to believe that the defendant could've been tied in to that operation as well".

"I object, your honor!" Mark exclaimed, realizing that Mr. McWhite had raised an inadmissible issue. Mark and Mr. McWhite crossed words, then Judge Adams banged his gavel on his desk and demanded, "Order in the court!" The judge realized that Mark was in the right, so he looked over at Promise and asked to hear her side of the story. All of the jurors fixed their eyes on her.

Promise and Mark had went over her alibi numerous times, so she promptly began, "Your honor, I would like to begin by saying that I was illegally apprehended and that all of the allegations against me today are frivolous. I am an author and all of my property was purchased with legal money that I was paid by my publisher, Mr. Andre Vasquez, who is seated in the courtroom today. I have, with me today, legal documentation to prove that I was paid $100,000 cash to sign to his company three years prior to my arrest. I also have legal documentation stating that all of my further payments were made with cash. That's why the Feds were unable to find any record of me being employed, because I never had to cash any checks. Also, I would like to add that I was terminated from my part-time job because of my arrest." When Judge Adams realized that Promise had fully stated her case, he asked Mark Nettles what he had to say. That's when Mark stood, "May it please the court?" Then he walked over to the judge's bench and handed him a copy of Andre's annual tax reports, and Promise's author/publisher agreement. The judge put on his reading glasses and began looking over the documents, as Mark attested to all of Promise's claims. Mark also carried a copy of the documents over to the jury panel, insisting that they all passed them around.

Mark had everyone's undivided attention as he was putting Mr. McWhite to shame, shining in his charcoal-gray two-piece Armani suit. Everyone was awed, and the jurors had begun to view Promise in a different light. Mark colored their whole perception of her, making her appear to be an innocent victim. He did his thing for almost twenty minutes, expounding on the embarrassment that Promise had faced due to her character being crucified through the media. Then the judge called for a 45-minute recess so that the jury could form a consensus.

As everyone evacuated the courtroom, Promise joined Mark, Andre, Xena, and Zaire in the hallway. They formed a huddle, so to speak, and Mark spoke quietly to them all as they waited for the elevator. "Promise, you did an excellent job and I'm almost sure that you're about to get an acquittal. I could see it in the judge's face. You all just go ahead and grab some lunch and we'll meet back up here in forty-five minutes"

Both couples left to grab a quick bite to eat from a local carry-out Chinese spot. Then Promise hurried back to the courthouse, careful not to risk being served a bench warrant. She knew that, at that point, the courts were liable to do anything that they could to take her down. Promise arrived back in the courtroom punctually, while everyone was filtering back in. She and Andre returned to their seats at Mark Nettles' table in front of the judge's bench. All of the jurors were in the jury booth, Mark had returned, and so had the District Attorney, the Fed agents, and the Attorney General. The only ones missing were the judge and the stenographer, who both entered the courtroom almost ten minutes later.

As Judge Adams proceeded to his bench, the court officer ordered the courtroom, "All rise". Then, Judge Adams took a seat and told everyone else to be seated. Once the courtroom was settled and everyone seemed ready to proceed, he cleared his throat and began. The entire courtroom was silent as he asked the jury to submit their verdict. That's when the bailiff walked over to receive a sheet of paper from the foreman of the jury, conveying it to Judge Adams. The judge took the sheet of paper, put on his reading glasses once again, and read their decision to himself. He glanced over at Mark Nettles who was wearing a confident smirk on his face. Judge Adams continued, reading verbatim from the sheet of paper, "In the case of Ms. Promise Heyward, indictment number 01-389, we the jury find the defendant......" The judge hesitated as if it burned him to the marrow in his bones to proceed. At that point, Promise's nerves were rattling like crazy. Then, "Not guilty", he stated conclusively.

Promise dropped a few tears of joy, feeling like a ton of bricks had been lifted from her shoulders. She rose to her feet, gave Mark a hug, and then gave Andre a hug and a kiss. That's when Xena and Antiwan walked over to their table. Promise picked up Zaire and kissed him on his cheek, while the prosecution stared angrily like they had taken the loss personal. Mark then shut his briefcase and whispered, jocularly, to Promise, "Let's get out of here before they get spiteful and try to serve you a warrant for tax evasion or something". Then, they all left the courthouse and both couples drove to Promise's apartment to hang out until it was time for Xena to pick her sons up from school. Mark and a few of his partners from the firm went to a local pub to have a few drinks and to celebrate his victory.

Mark decided to visit Murda and flaunt his victory on the next morning, since Murda never called him that Monday evening after Promise's trial. Murda's second bond reconsideration was coming up in two weeks. He had been living in his cell alone for almost three months, ever since Cool's parole officer revoked his sentence and sent him back to prison. Cool had to max-out the remaining time that he had on parole, plus his charges from the Dru Hill bust were still pending.

Mark explained, to Murda, that Promise's acquittal had given him some leverage in his case. He also said that he was confident that Murda would be granted a bond that time around, although it might've been expensive. Those words were like music to his ears because the cash was still pouring in profusely and his freedom was priceless. Mark also suggested that Murda could request a speedy trial as Promise did, now that he felt confident that he could win his case. Strangely, that was the least of Murda's concerns, since Mark leaked the fact that Promise was pregnant.

Promise had been running through Murda's mind day-in and day-out, for months, and confronting her face to face was his primary concern. That was paramount. He ordered Mark not to tell Promise or anyone else that he may be getting released, and he intended to do likewise. He wanted to come home like Jesus Christ on Easter Sunday morning and surprise everyone, including his Blood homies. The workers that he had running his crack spot in Park Heights were still fucking up, coming up short on his money every week. He couldn't wait to show his face on that side of town again, not only to get his business back intact, but to smack fire out of a few niggas who had been shitting on him like he was never gonna touch down.

Equally important to him was finding Andre and making sure that he was dealt with. He could've easily sent a few of his dogs to eat his food, but he wanted to do the honors. He felt like Andre had violated majorly by getting Promise knocked up and, secondly, by interacting with Zaire.

Murda spent the next two weeks practically growling at the window each night, anticipating the sweetest revenge. He still had a few ounces of weed and coke to sell so he decided not to have anymore brought in until he found out how his bond hearing was gonna turn out. He knew that if he was granted a bond, he would be released that very same day, if not that same hour. He had already decided that if any drugs were leftover when it was time for him to bounce, they would've been divided amongst all of the Bloods in his pod.

One week after Mark's visit, Murda received an unexpected letter from Promise. The return address was the same as the P.O. Box address that Redrum had found on the True Life Publishing website. Promise was writing him to let him know that she had won her case and that the courts were gonna return all of his property to her, including his cell phone and the $50,000 that was confiscated. She, being a good sport, said that she was gonna make sure that he received all of his property, even the 3 Series BMW that he had originally purchased for her.

Promise didn't want anything from him. She didn't know what he wanted her to do with all of his property so she asked him to write her back at the return address on the envelope. She also made it very clear that she was still in a relationship and that she wasn't harboring any hard feelings towards him. Also enclosed with the letter, were ten recent photos of Zaire. Little did Promise realize, that letter would do more harm than good, although that wasn't the desired effect.

19

DRY TEARS

With her court situation now behind her, Promise could finally begin touring to promote her book. Andre's booking agent had booked her a few radio interviews in the DMV area (D.C., Maryland and Virginia). She decided not to do any in-store book-signings until after her son was born. She had also decided to go on a maternity leave from Dick's and was spending a lot of time working on her next book, entitled Dry Tears. Dry Tears was gonna be the story of how she met Andre and discovered true love.

Andre hadn't changed the least bit since they started dating. He was still loving and kind, constantly surprising her with gifts, and he loved spending quality time with her and Zaire. Heartache seemed oceans away from Promise, and if she ever did feel uneasy about anything, he was her crying shoulder. Also, he accepted Zaire as his own son. Although Murda was negligent of his son, Andre encouraged that Promise always kept Zaire wary of whom his biological father was, and that she never bashed Murda in front of his son. That was something that he just didn't condone.

Promise still had her apartment out in Bowie, although she and Zaire had been spending many nights at Andre's house in Southeast, D.C. Promise and Andre couldn't stay away from each other for long, plus Zaire had become attached to Andre. Promise was actually waiting for Andre to pop the big question on her so that she could say "I do" without second-guessing.

That Sunday night before Murda's bond hearing, he didn't get a wink of sleep. That day, he had the barber to hook him up with a fresh cut and a clean shave so that he would look presentable before the judge. Winter and their two sons were going to be present in the courtroom for moral support, and Mark Nettles was gonna be there to speak in his behalf.

That night, Murda packed up all of his property as if he was certain that the judge was gonna give him a break that time around. All of that hardcore gangsta shit went out the window the next morning when Murda found himself on his knees, begging God to soften the judge's heart. His hearing was scheduled for 9:30 a.m. That morning, he put on a brand new long-sleeved thermal top to cover the tattoos on his arms. Plus, he threw on a pair of gold Prada frames that Erica had smuggled in for him.

When the dorm-officer's voice came over the intercom in his room, Murda was sitting on his bed, already fully-dressed. "I'm ready", he answered, and then the C.O. opened his cell door. That's when he walked over to the officer's station where there was an officer waiting for him with a pair of handcuffs and ankle chains in his hands. Murda was then cuffed and escorted to a courtroom down the hallway, along with a few other detainees from different pods.

When Murda looked at all of the other guys, they gave off a totally different image. Two of them had dreads and the others had afros and braids. None of them had taken the time out to shave or anything, causing Murda to stick out like a sore thumb. Another thing that distinguished him from all of the others was that none of them had legal representation, nor family members present for their moral support. Mark Nettles made his presence felt dressed all debonair in his tailored suit and his Gucci loafers.

Murda's case was the first case to be heard. He didn't recognize the judge because he'd never seen him before. He was a circuit judge from another county, so he probably knew very little about Murda's case, only what was written in the incident reports and his indictment papers. The judge probably also knew that he'd been denied a bond three times already.

Murda stood when he was called upon for his case to be heard. Mark stood next to him, waiting for the judge to speak his piece so that he could do all of the talking for Murda. Murda was nervous for the entire time. Mark explained that Murda had been in jail for over six months, having only one disciplinary, and was denied a bond thrice. He also explained that he had a family who needed him at home, directing the judge's attention to Winter and their two sons who were seated on the first row in the courtroom. He then mentioned that Murda didn't have any prior drug charges in his criminal jacket.

That particular judge had a personal disdain for drug offenders so he decided to give Murda a bond that he assumed he couldn't afford to pay. The bond was set for $100,000 cash or $300,000 surety. The other detainees gave Murda looks of pity, obviously unaware of the type of cash that he was playing with. Murda shook his head and sighed at the judge, pretending like the bond amount was too high. Then he sat down and waited on the officer to escort him back to his cell.

As soon as Murda walked back into his cell, he grabbed his cell phone from beneath his pillow and called his homie Bloodshot, the bail bondsman. Murda didn't want anyone to know that he was coming home so he told Bloodshot to pick him up and that he would pay him personally. Bloodshot agreed and said that he would be there around 12:00 that afternoon.

Murda didn't have that much product left, only about a half-ounce of weed and a few grams of coke. He flattened them both in a sheet of paper so that he could slide them under one of his Blood homies' cell-doors on his way out. He took the sim card out of his cell phone and stashed it inside of his mail because he had planned to take it home with him. He wanted to keep that same cell number instead of using the phone that the Feds had returned to Promise. He placed the actual phone inside of a brown paper bag that he had planned to throw into the garbage can by the officer's station. When he was done packing up everything that he'd planned to carry home with him, he waited patiently for Bloodshot to come through.

Murda, still fully-dressed, passed out on his rack while he was waiting on Bloodshot. As soon as the 12:00 count cleared, the dorm-officer's voice came over the intercom in his room, "Mr. Reed. Pack up, you're being released". Murda walked out of his cell and the officer was watching him closely so he slid the weed and the coke under one of his homies' doors, pretending like it was his telephone number. Then he said, "Call me when they let you out for rec tonight", loud enough for the officer to hear him. On his way to the officer's desk, he threw the brown paper bag into the garbage can. Then, he turned around to be handcuffed. That's when he was escorted to the Bookings area to be processed out, smiling every step of the way.

When he finally got released, Bloodshot was waiting for him in front of the jail, driving an all-black G Wagon Benz truck. Their first and only stop was at Winter's crib on Emerson

Avenue. That's when Murda went inside and retrieved $30,000 from his gun-stash in the stairs. Then he gave the cash to Bloodshot, reminding him to keep his mouth shut about him being out of jail. Murda spent that entire afternoon fucking Winter, smoking dippers and getting wasted on Patron. Then he made her run a few errands for him. He wanted her to swing by the T Mobile store to buy him another phone that would accept his sim card.

As soon as she returned with his phone, he called out to his workers in Park Heights. He was calling to schedule a Nine, pretending that he had supplied Bloodbath with some new product that he wanted to put on the market. He stressed that everyone needed to be there or be subjected to being demoted or replaced. Knowing that it would take at least twenty-four hours to rally everyone up, he scheduled the Nine for the following evening at 7:00, at the B-Hive. Then he called up all of the heads over his Westport, Cherry Hill and Dru Hill spots, ordering all of them to be there as well.

Bloodbath was the very last person to know about the meeting, still oblivious to the fact that Murda was home. Murda called Bloodbath around 5:00 p.m. the next day and told him to pick up the new product from Winter's crib around 6:00. Bloodbath arrived on cue and he was shocked to see Murda walk out of the house as he was parallel parking his truck out-front. As Murda approached the truck, empty-handed, Bloodbath then realized that Murda had lied about having some new product. When Murda hopped in, they exchanged pounds, then Murda gave him a heads-up on what to expect in their meeting. Not once did he apologize for lying. Pretending to be enthralled by Murda's cleverness, Bloodbath actually felt insulted that Murda didn't trust him to keep his secret. Murda didn't want anyone to know that he was home until the moment that he arrived at the B-Hive with Bloodbath. His success was near total, except for the fact that Bloodbath was on his cell phone with his wifey when he pulled up. As soon as he spotted Murda, he blurted out, "Oh shit, Murda's home".

When they arrived at the B-Hive, that entire block of Russelltown Road looked like a Big Tymers video. Parked out front were everything from drop-top Vettes, Benzos, Beamers and a few tricked-out SUVs. Murda, completely hidden behind the dark limo tint, smiled nefariously when he spotted one of his Park Heights workers named Gusto standing on the sidewalk. As soon as Murda opened his door and planted one foot on the ground, a few of the Bloods spotted him. Then everyone swarmed the truck to welcome him home. Everyone was pulling his dick, telling him how diesel he looked. Murda didn't display any type of emotion, holding a straight face and speaking very few words.

Everyone surrounded him like he was Nino Brown, as they all crossed the street to enter the B-Hive. Murda was lining Gusto up the entire time. Just as he was about to walk inside, he turned around and stole on Gusto, dropping him. The blood coursing through his veins was boiling-hot and he just couldn't resist it. While most of the others wondered what Murda's motive was, he ordered a few of them to pick him up off of the ground and bring him inside before the cops passed by.

Once inside, Murda didn't waste any time getting down to business. He unplugged the jukebox and made Spark turn off all of the televisions. Then he stood in the center of the floor and demanded everyone's full attention. First he spoke about how dissatisfied he was with the way that his Park Heights workers were running that spot. Among those numbers, he called out at least ten names of Bloods that he wanted to go in the paint. Going "in the paint" is when a Blood gets violated by being beaten for thirty one seconds by four or five other Blood members. There was no mercy to be shown and blows to the face and the head were not exempt. That day, a few of his workers lost their positions and some of them moved up in rank.

When the meeting was over, Murda returned to Winter's crib to relax and try to figure out a way to contact Promise. He had planned to contact her under the guise of him only trying to make arrangements for them to meet up so that he could recover all of his property. The gospel truth was that he just wanted to confront her face to face. His property was the least of his worries. His first effort to get at her was on the next day when he called the Dick's store, only to learn that she had taken a maternity leave. Subsequently, he mailed her a letter that was addressed to the P.O. Box address that she had given him. In that letter, he informed her that he was out on bond and that he was only writing to make arrangements for them to meet up. He also gave her his cell phone number, urging that she called him as soon as possible.

Being that Murda didn't provide a return address, Promise called him as soon as she received his letter. She called one morning from a blocked number, four days later. Promise kept their conversation brief, limited to the matter at hand. She told him that all of his vehicles were already parked at his house in Annapolis and that she had stashed all of his keys in the trunk of his Acura TL, along with his $50,000. Therefore, she only had that one trunk key in her possession. She also explained that, surprisingly, the Feds never even touched anything in the house when they seized it. They left everything as it was. She never mentioned that she had also taken his Hi-Point .380 from underneath his mattress. She suggested that he allowed her to mail the key to his house but he pretended not to trust that, claiming that the feds were likely to be monitoring all of his incoming and outgoing mail. He also implied that he didn't trust his key being in the hands of anyone else, countering her possible idea to try to find someone else to deliver the key to him.

Promise was paranoid about meeting with him, remembering his temper, and considering the fact that she was pregnant. Murda spoke as calmly as he could, being careful not to plant any fear in her. After a few minutes, Promise said, concisely, "Fine. I'll meet you tomorrow at 2:00 at the DMV in Glen Burnie, right across from the Giant's supermarket". Murda then tried to bring up Zaire, claiming that he needed to see him. She agreed to bring him along with her on the next day, and then she ended their conversation.

Promise chose to meet him at the DMV because she knew that there would be a few police officers around. There wasn't a shred of doubt in her mind that Murda was still feeling some type of way about her moving on, even though he seemed so nonchalant about it. Andre was at work that morning, so he wasn't around when Promise agreed to meet with Murda. When he swung by her apartment for dinner that evening, she explained to him what she had agreed to and that she was feeling uncomfortable about driving out to Glen Burnie alone.

Andre told Promise not to fret because he would take the day off and ride with her. Out of common respect, he had planned to remain in the car and watch them from a distance, making sure that Murda didn't get out of pocket. Andre had been waiting for the opportunity to actually see Murda anyway, after all of the stories that he'd heard about how he used to mistreat Promise. He wanted to whip his ass but, out of respect for Zaire, he chose not to confront him about it.

On the following day, around 1:00 p.m., Promise, Andre, and Zaire headed out to Glen Burnie in Andre's cream Jaguar XJ. They arrived at the DMV just a few minutes before Murda and Bloodbath arrived in the Escalade. Murda hopped out, dressed in a pair of blue True Religion jeans, a pair of all-black suede construction Timberlands, and a black wife-beater. He wanted to show off his biceps and his triceps. The only jewelry that he had on was a diamond and steel Audemars Piguet wrist watch. Promise retrieved Murda's key from her small Berkin bag, then she and Zaire walked towards him, meeting him at midway.

The first thing that he noticed was how huge her stomach was. Pretending not to be fazed by it, he received his key, then picked up Zaire. Zaire seemed to only remember him vaguely, as he was practically kicking for him to put him down. For the entire time, Promise kept her eyes on Zaire, deliberately avoiding eye contact with Murda. Realizing that Zaire wasn't gonna cheer up, Murda decided to spark an idle conversation with Promise. "So, that's your new boyfriend huh?", he asked sarcastically.

Andre, still seated in the driver's seat of his Jag, beamed in like a hawk, trying to read Murda's lips. Promise made it clear that she wasn't beat for his rap when she interjected, "Murda, you need to hurry up because I don't have all day. You said that you needed to see Za Za. Tell him what you wanted to tell him so that we can be on our way". Murda snickered, then he turned to get a better look at Andre. He gave Andre a cold stare so Andre returned that same stare, telepathically saying, "Try it". Murda must've gotten the message because he was the first to look away.

For Murda, that was the point when things really got upset. "The nerve of this nigga to grit on me", he thought. He played it cool and put Zaire back on his feet. Then he told Promise to call him later so that they could discuss Zaire's custody situation. Without giving an answer, Promise turned to walk away and returned to Andre's car. Murda hopped back into the truck with Bloodbath and they drove off while Andre still remained parked. Promise was strapping Zaire down in his car seat. As

Bloodbath cruised past Andre's car, Murda and Andre locked eyes once again. That time, Murda insinuated a gun with two fingers and pointed it at his own temple. Then he silently said "Pow", making it easy for Andre to read his lips. Promise had missed the gesture but she knew Murda, and she knew that a war was about to ensue.

For the entire ride back to Bowie, Promise kept looking behind them to assure that they weren't being followed. When Andre caught on to what she was doing, he told her to relax because Murda was no threat. She truly believed that Andre would thrash Murda if they fought head-up, but she also knew that Murda had enough yank to have Andre clipped off without having to raise one finger. Careful not to crush Andre's male ego, Promise simply replied, "I know baby."

20

DEATH WARRANT

Winter asked Murda, "What's wrong baby?" She had been making sexual advances at him for fifteen minutes, but he didn't seem to be in the mood. She even tried to give him some head and he refused it. Seeing Promise pregnant was hard for him to stomach. His pride was hurt and, furthermore, he was embarrassed because all of his haters now had some ammunition to use against him. He was like an insomniac for that entire night, seeing Promise in his mind every time that he closed his eyes. Winter couldn't put her finger on what it was that was troubling him so she left him alone to deal with it. She just turned on the television set and watched *Criminal Minds* until she fell asleep.

Murda laid in bed alongside Winter, watching the tube and finishing off his shot of Patron Silver. The more intoxicated he got, the more furious he became. After one final gulp, Andre's death warrant was as good as signed. Murda was just brainstorming to come up with a clever method to trap his kill. As he was flipping through the tv stations, one particular infomercial caught his attention. It was a late-night advertisement for the yellow pages. The spokesman said that the viewers could find out the phone numbers to some of their closest friends if they knew their addresses, or vice versa. All they had to do was visit the website, www.yellowpages.com.

Murda immediately went into his phone to re-open all of Redrum's older messages that had been saved on his sim card. He wrote down the address to Promise's apartment in Bowie. Since Winter had passed out, he decided to go downstairs and check out the website on Winter's desktop computer. He typed in Promise's address and, to his surprise, a telephone number popped up, matching that address. He immediately stored the number in his contacts, planning to call it on the next day just to make sure that it was official.

The next morning, Murda got the idea to drive out to Bowie, just to scope out Promise's apartment complex. His driver's license was temporarily suspended because of his pending drug charges. Plus, he was under scrutiny by the Feds so he didn't wanna do any driving. He decided to call Redrum to see if he would be willing to drive for him. Redrum never had a driver's license to begin with but he felt compelled to help Murda because of the 25 stacks that he had dropped on him, plus the bond money that he had kicked out. As far as he was concerned, Murda had a lifetime's insurance with him. When Redrum agreed, Murda told him to have Astria to drop him off at Winter's crib around 6:00 that evening. Around 8:00 that night, Murda and Redrum arrived in Heather Ridge Apartments, driving Winter's Altima.

When they arrived in the parking lot, Redrum immediately noticed that all of the lights in her apartment seemed to be turned off. Plus Andre's Lamborghini and his Jaguar were nowhere in sight. Redrum parked the car in an empty parking space near the corner of her building, and they decided to wait until the couple returned home. While waiting, Murda scanned the parking lot to see what the surveillance was like, just incase he chose to get it on with Andre right there in the parking lot. Murda then realized that that was the opportune moment to call her number and see whose voice would come over the answering machine's greeting.

Murda pressed *67 just before he called, so that his number would be restricted. To his surprise, Promise answered after the second ring, "Hello". Her voice caught Murda off guard so he remained silent, causing her to repeat herself more aggressively. Then Murda hung up the phone, still having not said one word.

It turned out that Promise was inside of the apartment for the entire time. She was in her bedroom, located in the back, packing her and Zaire's clothes so that they could go to Andre's house for the night. When Murda hung up in Promise's face, it startled her for a moment. She'd been feeling kinda paranoid ever since she saw Murda on the previous day. After a few seconds, she decided to laugh it off, assuming that Murda couldn't possibly have had her phone number. That's when she finished packing and prepared to leave.

Murda sat patiently, waiting for one of Andre's luxury cars to pull into the parking lot. As they were waiting, they both noticed the blinking headlights on a white Honda Civic, along with the sound of a car alarm being deactivated. That's when they spotted Promise and Zaire making their way to the car, with no trace of Andre. Murda noticed that Promise was looking all around for any potential danger so he and Redrum sunk into their seats to remain hidden until she drove off.

A few cars were filtering in and out of the complex. There were two cars in front of Promise and three cars behind her, as they were all about to leave Heather Ridge and merge into the ongoing traffic on English Oaks Avenue. That's when Murda ordered Redrum, "Follow that bitch". Redrum fell to the back of the line, keeping his eyes glued on the Honda Civic to see which direction Promise was gonna turn in. She made a right, in the direction of Interstate 95.

Redrum followed Promise, remaining a few cars behind her as she veered onto I-95 South. As they were driving, it started to drizzle. Promise still had no idea that she was being followed. When they crossed the Washington, D.C. line, Murda began to wonder if she was headed out of town. It seemed likely, considering the fact that she was carrying a small suitcase when she walked to her car.

It wasn't long before Promise was parallel parking her car directly in front of Andre's house on Pennsylvania Avenue. Redrum, still a sensible distance behind her, parked a few houses back so that she wouldn't notice them passing by her. Winter's Altima didn't have any tint at all. By then, the rain had totally ceased. As Promise was stepping out of her car, Andre walked out of his house in his bedroom shoes, a pair of HOBO sweatpants, a wife-beater and a du-rag. The first thing that Murda noticed was his muscular physique, assuming that he must've done some time before or was into body-building. His arrangement didn't seem pussy at all, contrary to the square-john description that Redrum had given of him.

It took everything inside of Murda not to blow his own cover and start busting at Andre as he watched Zaire run up the steps and lunge into Andre's arms. Then, just before they walked inside of the house, Promise approached Andre and tongue-kissed him right in front of Zaire. That put the icing on the cake, and the candles. Murda noticed that Andre had a few toys in his driveway: the Lambo, the Jag, and a silver E-Class. Plus, he had the Excursion parked directly behind Promise's car.

Murda knew that for any man to be living in Southeast, D.C. with that big crib and all of those fly cars, he had to have some type of means to protect them. Either he was gang-affiliated or he had already laid his murder game down flat. Otherwise, he would've been food in that part of town. Whatever the case was, Murda decided not to sleep on him, realizing that he wasn't gonna be an easy prey. As much as he wanted to run up in his crib right then and there, he was smart enough not to go out like a belligerent fool. The tags on the car were registered in Winter's name and address where he was resting his head at every night. All it would've taken was for one neighbor to rat him out and the cops would've been at Winter's crib before he made it back home that night.

Promise didn't return to her apartment until two days later. It was early that Saturday morning. She had dropped Zaire off at Xena's crib so that he could spend the day with her two sons. Promise had intended to rest for the entire day until Xena returned Zaire home around 6:30 that evening. It was roughly 9:00 that morning when Promise walked into her apartment. That time of morning was the most peaceful time of the day for her because most of her neighbors were either at work or still asleep. Her tempur-pedic mattress was screaming out her name as she turned the key to walk inside.

As she made her way down the hallway to crash out, she noticed that there was an awkward silence in the apartment. Even though nothing looked out of place, her intuition told her that something wasn't right. When she walked into her bedroom, she placed her purse on the floor beside her bed. Then she sat down on the bed to remove her shoes. And, that's when it happened....the element of surprise.

Murda walked into the bedroom, apparently drunk, scaring Promise half to death.

"Murda, what the fuck are you doing in my house?!" Promise snarled, sending a sharp pain to her stomach.

Murda gawked at her as if he'd expected a different reaction. Then he replied, "Relax baby. Stop acting all crazy, this is me".

"Don't baby me, get the fuck out...I'm calling the cops!" she barked, attempting to grab the telephone on the nightstand next to her. Before she could finish dialing 911, Murda's immediate reaction was to punch Promise in her face, causing her to drop the phone and collapse to the floor. Murda had practically knocked her unconscious and, when she hit the floor, she fell on her stomach hard enough to damage the fetus inside of her.

"See what you made me do?" asked Murda, hovering over her like a madman. Promise lingered in and out of consciousness, as everything seemed blurred and all of Murda's words sounded like they were dragging. Promise squinted, seeing a fuzzy image of Murda walking towards her. Still not responsive enough to put up any type of fight, Promise felt Murda turn her over on her back. Then she felt her pants being removed. Unable to speak audibly, she realized that Murda was trying to have sex with her. Still dazed, all that Promise could do was mumble "No… please". Unfortunately, the only person who could've possibly heard her cries was the child inside of her, who couldn't do anything at all to help her. In his intoxicated mind, Murda actually believed that he was about to make her fall in love all over again with his stroke.

As Promise became more conscious, realizing that she was being raped, all that she could do was distill tears. Eventually, her silent whimpering turned into yells and she began fighting with every fabric of her existence. Of course, her resisting proved unsuccessful as he was already inside of her. She was technically powerless against his manpower, forcing her to lie there and withstand the pain of him going in and out of her. As her cries became louder, he just covered her mouth with his hand and continued to pleasure himself. It went on for almost five minutes before Murda ejaculated his seed inside of her. Then he rose to his feet, leaving Promise lying on the carpet, crying as much as she could without increasing the pain in her stomach.

Watching Promise sprawled across the floor, Murda realized that he'd just crossed bounds that he wouldn't be able to return from. Without a doubt, she was gonna notify the cops as soon as she got the chance. In his drunken stupor, his instincts told him to restrain Promise. That's when he pulled the telephone cord out of the wall. Then he went into Promise's purse and grabbed her cell phone.

Confident that she wasn't going anywhere, he went into the kitchen to search for something to restrain her with. That's when he found some duct tape in the drawer. He hurried back into the bedroom where he found Promise still unmoved, groaning softly from the pain. By that point, Murda had sobered down a bit and was just as scared as she was. He was afraid of what might consequently happen to him. The first thing that he did was duct tape her mouth shut. Then he tied her down to a chair next to her bed, using her bed sheets and the telephone cord. He made sure that he tied strong knots when he tied her ankles to the legs of the chair, making it impossible for her to walk anywhere. He just placed her hands behind her back and duct taped her wrists together.

Murda had been waiting in Promise's apartment for over three hours. Redrum had dropped him off and was waiting on standby for him to call so that he could pick him up in Murda's Range Rover. He and another van carrying four other Bloods were parked down the block from Andre's crib, laying for him. Murda had given them strict orders to let him have it as soon as he walked out of his house. Promise played possum as Murda called Redrum up on speakerphone. She was just happy to still be alive, hoping that the worst part was over. In her mind, she hoped that Andre would come sweeping in to save her, even though she wasn't expecting him until later on that night after he got off work.

When Redrum answered, Murda said, "Yo homie, what's the prognosis?"

Redrum replied, "We're still waiting outside of the nigga's crib. Are you sure that he's in there?"

"What cars do you see parked out front?"

Redrum named all of Andre's cars and Murda confirmed, "Yeah, he's in there. As a matter of fact, come through and scoop me up real quick. I wanna burn the nigga myself".

"And, what if he comes out before we make it back?"

"Then the other homies will just have to put the work in. But, come right now my nigga."

Murda realized that he had fucked up big time and he was uncertain about what he was gonna do to prevent Promise from involving the police. He was starting to regret hurting her but the damage was already done. One thing for sure and two things for certain, Andre had a date with destiny. Things had gotten too deep and he couldn't dare be the one spared when it was all said and done.

When Promise overheard Redrum naming all of Andre's cars, she realized what was about to transpire. All that she could do was visualize the love of her life being ambushed as soon as he walked out of his house to go to work at 11:30, only one hour later. Murda paced back and forth in Promise's bedroom for almost thirty minutes, frequently looking out of the window for police. When he finally spotted his Range parked out front, he kissed Promise's face as she continued to play possum. Then he told her that he would be back later and walked out of the bedroom, shutting the door behind himself. As soon as the door slammed, tears began to flow down Promise's face as she feared for what was about to happen to Andre.

Redrum and Murda arrived back on Pennsylvania Avenue as Andre was inside of his house getting dressed for work. He had no idea that the wolves were outside waiting for him. Andre walked out of the house, dressed in a two piece suit by Alexander Wang and a pair of Mauri loafers. He was carrying a black briefcase. He walked towards his Jaguar, paying very little attention to his surroundings. Andre had his back turned as he was getting into the driver's seat. That's when he heard a voice coming from a few yards behind him, "What's poppin' now nigga?" As Andre turned around to see who the owner of the voice was, Murda brandished his .45 and shot at him, grazing his head.

Andre's street instincts kicked in immediately, as he reached for the 40 cal. that he kept in a holster on his side. Before he could grab it, Redrum had hit him in the arm with a bullet from his .38. Andre's neighbor and right-hand man named Jerome heard the shots and rushed outside to Andre's aide, carrying an AR-15. Andre, now on the ground, had managed to back out the 40 cal. and he started firing recklessly in the direction of Murda and the five other Bloods in his driveway. He caught Murda in the leg as the shots continued in his direction. Andre was making his way back towards the car noticing that a few shots had riddled the side of it. When Jerome recognized what was going on, he started unloading on all six of them.

When Murda and his squad heard the AR-15 sounding off, they all started to retreat towards the van. Andre, leaking from one arm, followed in pursuit, trying to get a clean shot at Murda. When he felt confident that he wouldn't miss, he stopped running, aimed steadily, and fired. Murda was only a few steps away from his truck when he dropped from Andre's shot to the neck. Jerome continued to shoot at the four others who were making their way back to the van. Everyone had been hit with the exception of Jerome.

As Redrum ran to the passenger's side of the truck to help Murda get inside, Andre caught him in his back. Jerome was still lighting up the van as they were speeding off with the back door still opened. Holding his wounded arm, Andre walked up on Murda and Redrum who were both lying on the ground, practically defenseless. With no compassion, Andre emptied the rest of his clip into both of them.

The air reeked of gun smoke and the sound of police sirens seemed to be getting closer. At that very moment, it was almost like Andre had heard a voice in his head, saying Promise's name. He realized that that was only his intuition warning him to rush to her aide. That's when he hopped into his Lamborghini and backed out of the driveway as fast as he could. Then he sped en route to Promise's apartment, sweating and badly wounded. When Promise didn't answer her cell phone, he floored the accelerator with no regards for the state troopers on I-95. As he got closer to her apartment, he called 911 and told the dispatcher to send the police to Promise's apartment because she was in danger.

Andre arrived there before the cops did so he hurried to Promise's door, reloading his gun with an extra clip that he kept in the console of his car. He began to panic when he realized that her front door was unlocked. That's when he quietly turned the door knob and crept in with his gun drawn. He knew immediately that something was wrong because he noticed Promise's car parked in the parking lot, but there wasn't a sound to be heard inside of the apartment. Andre took soft steps down the hallway as he headed towards Promise's bedroom, expecting to find her slain. Before attempting to open her bedroom door, he placed his ear on the door to hear if anyone was inside. When he didn't hear anyone, he slowly turned the door knob and opened the door.

Before he could even blink, Andre was hit with two swift shots to the chest from a Hi-Point .380. Promise had shot Andre by accident, assuming that he was Murda. When she realized that he wasn't, it was too late. The love of her life was now bleeding to death on her bedroom floor. Promise was traumatized. Still strapped to her chair by her ankles, she was unable to do anything besides cry and watch his life wither away.

Shortly before Andre arrived, Promise had painstakingly broken loose from the duct tape around her wrist. She removed the tape from over her mouth and was able to retrieve the gun which she had stashed under the mattress right next to her. She was in the process of trying to loosen the knots that were tied tightly around her ankles when she overheard Andre entering through the front door. That's when she was forced to stop trying, so that she could arm herself.

The cops arrived at Promise's apartment almost five minutes after she had shot Andre. When she heard them knocking at the front door, her heart began to thud as she was expecting it to be Murda. When no one answered, they rushed in, 6 officers-deep. All of them had their guns drawn. When Promise heard their police radios getting closer, she cried out, "In here, hurry!". They immediately noticed Andre's body lying stiff in the doorway, then they spotted Promise's gun on the floor. Two of the officers rushed over to free Promise, while one of the officers checked Andre's neck for a pulse. When he didn't feel a pulse, he placed his finger under Andre's nostrils to see if he was breathing. That's when they realized that Andre was dead.

The ambulances arrived shortly afterwards. When the officers noticed Promise's swollen eye, and the fact that she was pregnant and restrained, they automatically concluded that there was some foul play involved. Promise and Andre were both carried away in separate EMS Units, although Andre was practically pronounced dead on the scene. Promise wasn't questioned by the investigators until after she received immediate medical attention.

EPILOGUE

"Good evening. A Washington, D.C. man named Andre Vasquez was found dead earlier today in the Heather Ridge Apartment complex in Bowie. Deputies from the Bowie Police Department say that they were responding to a call that was made by Mr. Vasquez, just minutes before he was killed. According to investigators, the 32 year- old victim called to report that his girlfriend, Ms. Promise Heyward, was in danger. When the police arrived on the scene, Ms. Heyward was found restrained to a chair in her apartment, badly wounded and noticeably pregnant. Mr. Vasquez was lying dead in her doorway as a result of multiple gunshots. Investigators say that Ms. Heyward accidentally shot Mr. Vasquez, mistaking him to be her ex-boyfriend, Mr. Joseph Reed out of Baltimore. Mr. Reed was one of the bodies that were found dead today in the Southeast section of Washington, D.C. The other body was a man named Richard Gist, who was also from the Baltimore area. Residents from Pennsylvania Avenue told police that both men were caught in a spray of bullets that were fired by unknown assailants. Mr. Reed had allegedly raped Ms. Heyward just hours before he was killed. Ms. Heyward was rushed to the Bowie Health Center and she is listed in stable condition. Her unborn child is also said to be fine. The information that she gave the police helped to solve the unsolved shootings on Pennsylvania Avenue. The investigators deemed Mr. Vasquez's murder as totally accidental, and

Ms. Heyward will not be charged. I'm Wanda Draper, and this is WBAL, Channel 11 News. Goodnight Baltimore"

THE END

Please turn the page for a preview of
Journey by Now Born

CHAPTER ONE

As we flew over the Atlantic Ocean, I must've had a million thoughts racing through my brain. I was so zoned-out that I was able to block out my noisy brigade of approximately 300 troops, all shouting and celebrating the fact that we had survived the war and were returning home to our families. Deep down I was happy to be returning back to Harlem but I didn't have a lot of enthusiasm about it. I had a window seat and my eyes were watching the ocean for the majority of the flight back to the states. For some reason, I thought about the stories that my father used to tell me about the Trans-Atlantic slave trade. Flying over that ocean, it was almost like I could hear the cries of my ancestors who were killed on those slave ships, then thrown overboard to be devoured by the sharks.

Those fifteen months in Iraq had to be the longest fifteen months of my entire life. I had so many close brushes with death, and I lost quite a few comrades. I'll never forget the day when the Iraqis launched seventeen bombs which landed into our camp. We were outside working on our trucks and suddenly we heard the explosions. Most of us took cover under cement barriers and survived. All that we could hear were sirens as we hid ourselves, praying that the attack was over. Over thirty of my soldiers were killed during that bombing. I had a supervisor position since I was a sergeant. I stayed prayed up for the entire time as I traveled throughout that desert with my guys, trying to keep our shot group tight. We stayed low whenever those bombs landed into our camp.

Those Shiite Muslims are no joke. I can remember numerous times when they destroyed whole trucks with their I.E.D.'s (improvised explosive devices), killing no less than ten soldiers at a time. At one point, I lived really close to Saddam Hussein's palace. I was appalled at the fact that the rest of his country seemed to be living in hell-living without electricity, very little food, and there was garbage everywhere. Meanwhile, Saddam's palace was decked out with everything from gold toilets to marble floors and countertops. I realized then that it wasn't so terrible being an American. As a soldier in the United States Army, I was taught that our purpose for fighting in that war was to liberate the Iraqi people from the tyranny of their leader, Saddam. In fact, we referred to the war as Operation Iraqi Liberation. Almost naturally, I noticed that this was merely just an acronym for the word "oil", which everyone knows was a major factor in the war.

For some reason, those Iraqis didn't seem to want our help. They wanted us out of their country and they made that abundantly clear. Most of my soldiers were deployed out there for no less than fifteen months, some without any contact with their families. One of my comrades committed suicide because his wife divorced him while he was fighting in the war. I also watched quite a few soldiers lose their minds and I'm almost certain that they'll be shell-shocked for the rest of their lives.

I was also affected by the war. Before this war, I had never killed a man. Now, my body count is in the double digits and every single one of my victims was a total stranger. At heart, I knew that killing those men, women, and children was wrong but I rationalized it by telling myself that I was actually a hero. Strangely, even more so, something else was troubling me.

Just like many other soldiers, I had lost contact with my woman when I was deployed to Iraq. Her name was Lafayette. Lafayette had given birth to my first child about 4 months before I got deployed. I knew that I would be going off to war soon so, when our daughter was born, I decided to name her Journey. Journey was really light-skinned when she was born but, after a couple of months, she developed a mocha complexion like mine. She also had brown eyes like mine. Most of her other features resembled Lafayette's.

I really didn't understand why Lafayette chose not to correspond with me while I was overseas. I had always treated her like royalty when we were together. Although we weren't married, we were still an item. We lived together in a two-bedroom apartment in the section of Harlem called Morningside. I was the sole provider when we were together. Even while I was overseas, I'd had it set up online where the payment for our rent and our Con Edison bill came directly out of my checking account each month.

The only person who wrote to me in Iraq was my mother. She wrote me at least once a month. She and my father lived Upstate New York in Troy. She told me that Lafayette used to visit her frequently when I first got deployed. She even allowed Journey to stay with my parents for two months during that following summer. My mother became really attached to her only grandchild during those two months. She's really heavy in the church so they held Journey's christening at her church in Troy. My mother took Journey to church with her every Sunday, and she was showing her off all over town. When Lafayette picked Journey up at the end of the summer, my mother had bought lots of clothes and shoes for our daughter to take back to the city with her. Lafayette seemed to be acting strangely towards my mother that day, and my mother hadn't heard from her since then.

Our plane was scheduled to arrive at the John F. Kennedy Airport in approximately one hour and all that I could think about was confronting Lafayette. I had suspicions that she had stepped out on me because I'd seen it happen so many times to some of the other soldiers who were in my camp. I even passed up on the opportunity of a lifetime just to come back home and confront Lafayette. While in Iraq, I received a contract offer to stay overseas and do a contractor job in Iraq, Baghdad and Kuwait. Me working overseas meant tax free money. I would've been working as a civilian and the starting pay would've been $110,000 a year. I could've worked there for two years and been set for life. Had Lafayette been writing and keeping me informed on how she and Journey were holding up, that's exactly what I would've done.

When we arrived at JFK, I rushed outside and hailed the first yellow cab that I spotted. There was something refreshing about the pungent smell of the pollution in the air, and it felt good to be back in NYC. Without hesitation, I ordered the Gypsy cab driver to take me uptown to Harlem. Lafayette had no idea that I was coming home and I couldn't wait to see the expression on her face when I popped up at the door. I had already said in my mind that if another man was in our apartment, I was going to break him up without asking any questions.

When we arrived in Harlem, it was in the early evening darkness. I told the cab driver to drop me off near the corner of 114th Street and 8th Avenue. I didn't want to pull up on our block in a cab because that would've drawn too much attention. I decided to walk to Morningside, which was only two blocks away. I was still dressed in my B.D.U.'s, carrying my green duffel bag by the shoulder strap. It was in the blistering cold of January so I was wearing a black North Face jacket with the hoodie pulled over my head. Even in uniform, I wasn't afraid to walk the Harlem streets alone at night. I grew up in that area so I felt right at home.

When I arrived on our block, there were only five or six people walking on the sidewalk, and two or three people sitting on their stoops. They were all unfamiliar faces and none of them seemed to had recognized me. Once on the stoop of my building, I dialed the number to our apartment so that Lafayette could buzz me in. She never answered so I buzzed our next door neighbor, an elderly Puerto Rican woman named Ms. Gloria. When she realized that it was me, all that she could say was, "Ahh…dios mios", meaning "oh my God" in Spanish. She buzzed me in so I snatched the entrance door open quickly because I knew that it would've automatically locked back in a few seconds. When I arrived on the fifth floor, which was the top floor, Ms. Gloria was waiting for me at the top of the stairs. As soon as she spotted me, she opened her arms and welcomed me to a warm embrace.

To be continued….

THE FIERY FURNACE

DUAL OPPOSITES

MOVING TARGET Pt.2: VICE VERSA

NOTES

NOTES

NOTES

NOTES

www.ingramcontent.com/pod-product-compliance
Lightning Source LLC
Chambersburg PA
CBHW051824090426
42736CB00011B/1640